"In my role as a clinical psychologist, I have treated patients suffering from childhood trauma for over thirty years. Letha's *Pulling up Dandelions* is an honest, uplifting story about injury, pain, hope, and healing as it unfolds over a year of purposeful redemption. Her focus, determination, insight, and transparency are beautifully expressed. Her methods range from the expected (therapy and provocative reading) to the surprising ("redeeming ladies" and spiritual integration) and are wonderfully effective. I recommend her story to those who are haunted by childhood trauma, especially abandonment, and who seek to redeem that which was lost."

— David Agnor, PhD
Clinical Psychologist

"An inspiring and truly vulnerable journey towards healing and redemption that brings hope to the broken heart of my own inner child."

— Katy Ham
Licensed Mental Health Counselor

"*Pulling Up Dandelions* is a thoughtful reflection on a journey of healing and hope. Letha offers a model for redeeming a difficult past to build a healthy and fulfilling future."

— Candi Talbott
Educator

"A story of courage and determination to overcome deep and painful emotional wounds. This is a faith journey that will help many others."

— David Kern
former reporter and editor for *The Columbian*

"I was inspired by Letha's perseverance and fierce commitment to reclaiming her adolescence and learning the beauty and love of healthy relationships for her todays and tomorrows. A great read and reminder that it's never too late to heal, love, forgive and to trust."

— Shauna McCloskey
Therapeutic Specialty Courts Coordinator

"Turning toward our story is both the most painful and the most transformative thing we can do. Brandenburg bravely and lovingly shares her process of engaging her traumatic past in order to heal and redeem what was lost. This book is a tender invitation to those on a healing journey to move toward truth, scary as that may be, so they, too, might be set free."

— Renee Thompson
Licensed Mental Health Counselor

Pulling up Dandelions

A Woman's Journey
to Redeem Her Adolescence

Letha Brandenburg

Cover design by Madison Phillips

Interior design by Sarah Barnum

Author photo by Sheri Backous

ISBN 979-8-218-11528-9 (paperback)

979-8-218-11529-6 (e-book)

Printed in the United States of America

Contents

For my grandson, Ferris

1

Left on the Curb

April 1972

"Do you think she's coming?" Mark leaned down to pick up a pebble and toss it across the street. "We're going to be late for the game."

I assured my little brother that Mom had promised to pick us up right after she got off work from her part-time job at Montgomery Ward. "She'll be here. She's only twenty minutes late. Mom told me she wouldn't have a lot of time, so we're supposed to wait right here on the curb."

We lived on the west side of town in an older neighborhood lined with quaint Cape Cod houses and colorful bungalows built in the early 1930s. A public sidewalk connected the family homes, block after city block. Our street had the quiet setting of an older neighborhood and was free from much automobile traffic. It was a safe place for two kids to sit on the curb and wait.

The sun was warm on my back—a welcome relief from the rainy and cold Washington winter—as Mark and I sat, shoulders touching, in front of our house. I was just seventeen months older than my brother, but we couldn't have been more different. I was thirteen, blond and lanky, and Mark was eleven years old, stocky with freckles and brown hair. I was the thoughtful, serious type, and he was silly and carefree. I was content to wait a bit longer, but he was getting frustrated.

"Maybe she had to work late," he said, standing and kicking at pebbles.

"She'll be here," I reassured him. I rested my elbows on the grassy median that separated the street from the sidewalk, reaching over to pluck a few dandelions scattered in the grass. "We've got an hour before the game starts. Even if she's a little bit late, we'll still make the first pitch."

It was a perfect day for a baseball game, and my older brother Joey was playing that afternoon. Joey was seventeen months older than me. My two brothers and I were the three youngest children of eight. It was just the three of us living at home with Mom and Dad—the rest of our siblings were married or had moved out of the house.

Our family loved baseball. I especially loved going to ball games with Mom. It seemed she was happier at the ball field. I liked spending time with her there because she wasn't distracted. It felt like "our" time. While Mom scoped out the best spot on the bleachers, I'd head over to the concession stand to get licorice for the two of us and a cup of coffee for her. When I'd ask if she wanted anything in it, she would say, "Just put your finger in it, honey. That will sweeten it up." She was the ultimate baseball fan—you know, the one who kept score in her own scorebook and yelled a time or two at the umpire to let him know that he needed new glasses. She taught me how to keep score too. I was named Letha, after my mom, so she'd always have me fill in our name on the scorekeeper spot. We sat together on the bleachers with our scorebook and sharpened pencils, eating red licorice. Baseball games, springtime, and hanging out with my mom—a day couldn't get much better.

But on this particular day, Mom never showed up. Thirty more minutes passed, and Mark and I realized we should probably find another way to the ballpark. We figured Mom must have stayed late at work. I went into the house, made a couple of calls, and we hitched a ride to the park. Mark and I sat together on the bleachers and continued to wait. No Mom. Dad didn't show up either, so after the game the three of us kids found another ride home. We didn't have cell phones back in the 1970s, so if you didn't have access to a landline, you couldn't be reached at all.

When we got home Dad was there, but Mom still hadn't come home from work. It was pretty late by this time, and I started to worry. *Where is Mom?* The four of us scrounged around the kitchen, looking for something to eat. We threw together some bologna sandwiches and sat down at our yellow Formica kitchen table for a late dinner.

We were still sitting around the table when the phone rang at 8:00 p.m. Joey answered it. It was Mom. I couldn't hear what she said to him, but I watched Joey's face. He went white, didn't say but a couple of words, and then hung up. We stopped eating and waited. I stood up and took a couple of steps toward Joey. I could tell something was wrong by the look on his face. He said with a shaky voice, "That was Mom. She's not coming home." He continued, although I could tell he didn't want to. "She said she has a boyfriend, and she's leaving to go live with him."

Time stood still. Nothing made sense. Moms don't leave. And moms don't have boyfriends.

I started to tremble, and panic washed over me. I took a couple of steps back, reached for my chair, and collapsed. My heart pounded and the room started spinning. I closed my eyes so I wouldn't have to look at my brothers. I started to cry, and then I heard my brothers crying too.

My dad wasn't equipped to handle three fearful, weeping children. He was receiving the painful news for himself and was in shock and disbelief. His wife of thirty-two years had just left him. I was too consumed with my own fear and heartbreak to even consider his feelings. The four of us were all in our own heads, feeling our own feelings, or already trying to figure out how to not feel.

None of us said a thing for quite some time. Dad finally reached for me and helped me stand. "Come here, kids." He pulled us in for an awkward group hug, trying to make us feel a little better. He said with a cracking voice, "It will be okay. Everybody head to bed now. We'll be okay." So, we did what you do when you can't and don't know how to process pain. We turned off the lights and went to our rooms.

We lived in a two-story house with a basement. The boys' bedroom was in the basement, Mom and Dad's was on the main floor, and my room was upstairs. We all picked up our pain and dragged it to the different parts of the house. I climbed the stairs, carrying the weight of the world. Before then, I'd never known a pain so heavy. I had to tell myself to pick up my feet as I lugged myself up each stair like I was carrying a backpack filled with heavy books. I found my bed, laid down fully clothed, and sobbed into my pillow.

Laying there, I didn't cry out to God or even whisper a prayer like I had most nights up to that point in my life. I felt so alone, like I'd been abandoned by everyone, even God. My faith just didn't make sense to me. I'd been raised in a home with Christian beliefs and values, and, with one phone call, those values seemed to have disappeared. One minute I was standing on a firm and warm foundation; the next minute my footing was shaky and cold.

I went in and out of sleep all night. I'd drift off for a bit, then wake remembering. I replayed my brother's words over and over again: *Mom's not coming home.* The terrible reality birthed an ocean of worry in me that night. I went from an affirmed thirteen-year-old with the normal cares of an adolescent to a rejected teenager with concerns beyond my years. My confused and fearful mind raced. *What will happen to us? Who is going to take care of us? How is Dad going to handle this? How does a family make it without a mom? Why didn't Mom love me enough to stay?*

Morning finally came. Dad called up the stairs to make sure I got up for school. I imagine he didn't want to have to look at us before he left for work. The boys and I got ourselves ready, ate some breakfast, and walked out the door to catch the bus. Business as usual . . . but none of it was. Nothing was the same after that. Not for me, not for my brothers, and not for my dad. It never was again.

It's Not Too Late

November 2015

My husband, Barry, stood outside, taking in the view of the Lewis River from the deck of our two-year-old home in southwest Washington. We had affectionately named it "The Little River Lodge." It was a cold but sunny November morning, and he was dressed for golf in black and gray plaid slacks and a Nike pullover. I leaned out the door off the kitchen and asked, "Are you sure you don't want me to make your lunch? You guys will need to eat something if you're playing eighteen holes."

"We'll be fine, honey. We'll get a sandwich on the turn." Barry came in and headed to the garage to load his clubs. Bailey, our blond, long-haired dachshund, started barking, announcing Bennett's arrival as the front door opened.

Bending down, Bennett made the little bird-chirping sound he always greeted her with. "Hey, Bailey, how are you, sweet girl?" She jumped all over him. Her eyes were getting older, but her ears always recognized his voice. Bennett looked up. "Hey, Mom, how are you?"

"I'm alright. I'm glad you guys get to play golf today. Did you layer up? It's sunny, but it's going to be cold out there."

"Yes, Mom. I have another layer in my bag."

"Did you eat some breakfast? There's an extra egg and some toast here."

"Yep. I'm good."

"Hey, Ben," Barry said, coming in from the garage. "Ready to roll? I'd love to hit a bucket of balls before we tee off." Barry came over and gave me a kiss goodbye. "See you in about four hours, hon."

"Okay, you guys have a great time."

I walked over to the front of the house and stood at the window, watching them drive off. "My boys"—as I called them—were taking a much-needed break from their work at the law firm. Bennett had married his childhood sweetheart and now was interning for Barry at the law firm while finishing his law studies. Barry and I always thought we wanted a little girl, until Bennett came along. Raising him had been a great adventure and a perfect fit for me. After all, I'd been taking care of boys for a long time. Life had treated me well. It seemed, from the outside looking in, that I had escaped the effects of being a child of abandonment. But I was wrong.

Though it had been many years since Mom had left, the wounds of my past were beginning to bubble up to the surface in ways I couldn't ignore. A day at home to examine my thoughts and reflect on what I was feeling was just what I needed. I settled in a chair by the fireplace and picked up the book from the side table that I'd been reading. *Changes That Heal*, by Dr. Henry Cloud.[1] I flipped open to the chapter where I'd left off earlier in the week. Dr. Cloud explained how the source of adult pain often lies buried in behavioral patterns that began in childhood. I understood that concept and was ready to look at my buried pain.

I laid the book down, pulled out a journal and a pen, and wrote five pages about the years I took care of Dad and the boys. From the time I was thirteen until I got married at twenty-one, I always felt a great deal of responsibility for them. As I wrote, I realized even after I married, I struggled to let go of the need to keep my siblings close. I planned the gatherings, remembered their birthdays, and was the "glue" that kept my family together. When Bennett came along, I transferred that deep need to care for someone from my brothers to my son.

I shifted in my chair, put my journal down, and kept reading. Dr. Cloud said that emotional healing requires some pretty important ingredients, the first being **truth**. I had a natural tendency to deny the truth about myself and my past. I protected myself by avoiding the truth, or at least I thought I did. I recalled the movie, *A Few Good Men*.[2] In a heated courtroom interrogation, Kaffee says he wants the truth, to which Jessup barks, "You want answers? You want the truth?" Then he shouts, "You can't handle the truth!" I was like that. Truth uncovered things, and I had chosen to hide and stay covered up rather than admit the truth and unmask the painful stories of my childhood.

I kicked off my slippers and tossed the faux fur throw aside. I couldn't tell if I was feeling overheated because of the fireplace or the reality of what I was reading. I had lived an entire lifetime subtly denying the truth because I thought I couldn't handle it. I didn't understand how important my story was. At fifty-six years old, I was beginning to see that truth was the answer.

Grace was the second ingredient necessary for healing, according to Dr. Cloud. He defined grace as unearned love and acceptance. It's the kind of love where you can be exactly who you are. You don't have to hide your thoughts or feelings; you don't need to perform or please; you don't need to do anything to be loved. Someone knows the real you, and they love you anyway. I understood the need for truth and grace to heal, not only regarding my relationships with others, but more importantly, my relationship with myself. I saw where I was harsh and judgmental with myself because of mistakes I'd made (a little too much truth).

I looked up from reading and stared into the mesmerizing flames for a few minutes. *I'm going to have to extend more grace to myself as I begin to tell myself the truth.* I needed to learn to accept where I was and how I got there. I wanted to become curious about my behavior and my thinking instead of judging myself so harshly.

The third and most critical ingredient, according to Dr. Cloud, was **time**. I'd heard things like "time heals" and "time eases the pain," but this was different. To experience deep healing, I needed time joined together with truth and grace. Without those key ingredients, I had just passed through time without growing. I reached over, picked up my pen, and underlined that sentence. I passed through time without growing. When my mom left, I was removed from time and became an adult overnight. Instead of living the life of a teenager, I took care of my dad and brothers as a mother would have done. I became a little adult, in essence, never experiencing my teenage years.

Because of the trauma of being abandoned by my mom, I didn't get to work out my adolescent struggles—which left me subject to some inadequacies as an adult. However, Dr. Cloud also offered hope in the words of his book. He said because time is experience, I could influence any past aspect of myself in the present. It was never too late to open up to those who loved me and cared about my development. It wasn't too late for me to enter back into time and allow truth and grace to redeem it. I could use my current relationships to provide the nurturing and companionship I needed as a teenager.

I was so captivated by the concept of entering back into time that I didn't realize how much time had passed until I heard the garage door go up. Barry and Bennett walked through the back door, laughing. I knew they must have played well.

I looked up from my book. "How was your round?"

Barry answered with a chuckle, "Let's just say this, the worst day of golf beats the best day of work."

"Uh oh, that bad, huh?"

"No, we did okay. We both shot in the eighties. It wasn't the best round of our lives, but how can you complain when you get to play golf with your son on a sunny weekday in November?"

"I'm glad you guys had fun."

Barry nodded. "This isn't so bad either," he said, gesturing to my cozy chair by the fire.

"No, it isn't," I said with a smile. "I haven't moved from this spot since you left. I've been reading this fascinating book about what it takes to truly heal."

"Sounds interesting," Bennett said, setting his golf clubs against the wall and coming to sit in the chair next to me.

I gave them a short summary of Dr. Cloud's concept of time and healing. "It reminds me of your addiction recovery clients," I said to Barry. One of the most gratifying parts of his legal work was defending clients in our county's therapeutic drug court program. He advocated for people journeying through substance abuse recovery, many of whom had begun using drugs and alcohol in their early teens. This form of stagnation, being taken out of time, was true for them too. Their emotional development likely stopped at the age they began to escape life through drug abuse, some as early as nine or ten. They hadn't grown because they hadn't participated in life since then.

"Your clients chose to step out of time," I told him. "But I didn't. I was pushed out of time by someone else's decision."

Barry came over and sat on the hearth next to my chair. I could tell he was curious about what I was saying. "Interesting, hon. I'd never considered that you were pushed out of time like my drug court clients were."

Bennett nodded as Barry and I spoke. He knew many of the stories of my childhood, and we'd talked about them while he was pursuing his psychology degree. I was a great case study. Now, I could tell he was invested in my quest to heal by his quiet attention. When we finished, he responded.

"That's an important aspect of oneself I studied in my psych classes. There are critical developmental experiences we need to have growing up." He took off his golf hat and tousled his sandy-blond hair. He walked over to the fridge and filled up a glass of water, then came back and sat down. "Do you want to hear more?"

"Absolutely," I said, with a little lump in my throat.

"It's easy to identify the point when you got pushed out of time. Because time is experience, do you know when you could have stepped back into time for yourself? When I was thirteen. You could have relived your adolescence with me and reclaimed it for yourself."

I choked back tears as I considered this revelation. "Wow, Ben, I didn't know. I wish I'd done that." It would have been the perfect time to do that. When I was living those years as a loving mom of an adolescent, I could have processed the pain and the reality that I didn't have a mom who cared for me like I cared for Bennett. I didn't have a mom who sacrificed time, energy, and love for me. I didn't have a mom who delighted in my growth and adventures of becoming a young adult, and I didn't have a mom who was attuned to my feelings and cared to know my heart.

He could see me getting emotional, but he didn't seem uncomfortable. "Mom, you didn't do that because it would have been too painful, and you would have needed to come to terms with your pain. The easier option was to push that pain down again and again." Then he said something I would never forget. "So, you just kept taking care of me,

14

Dad, and our home and doing what you needed to do and what you'd been doing since you were a kid, in order to feel in control. I think we all make sacrifices to the detriment of our healing in order to keep control."

Bennett reached over and put his hand on mine. "I've got to get going, Mom, but I'm excited to hear more about what you'll do with this."

We stood, and he gave me a long hug before I walked him to the door. He turned as he reached his car in the driveway and said, "Mom, it's not too late."

It's not too late. I may have missed my opportunity to reclaim my childhood while Bennett was a teenager, but I hadn't lost it altogether. I was serious about healing, eager for truth and grace to transform me, and I was hopeful about the possibility that I really could recover the time that was lost. Now I just had to figure out how I was going to do that. How was I going to create "good time" and redeem my adolescence? I wasn't sure, but I was beginning to think it wasn't too late.

3

One Word Can Change Your Life

R uth was my best friend, until she wasn't. Ruth and I met through mutual acquaintances. Our relationship became emotionally intimate even from our first meeting. She asked me when we initially met for coffee if she could "be there for me" and offered her support and friendship without any expectation in return. I was hooked. I was attracted to the thought of being cared for without expectation. She followed through with her offer and immediately became an extremely important part of my life.

Ruth was connected and committed to every area of my life: me, my family, and my work. If I needed her for anything, she was there, just as she had promised. She became as faithful a friend to me and Barry as we had ever known. She provided the unconditional love and nurturing I'd always wanted and needed.

Fifteen years into our friendship, Ruth began to spend time with a different circle of friends and explore new experiences apart from me and my family. Feelings of rejection returned with a vengeance as if it were 1972 again. Shock, fear, and panic overwhelmed me similar to when I was thirteen years old. I knew my emotional response was unhealthy and inappropriate, but it took me time to realize that her choice to pursue other friendships acted as a trigger to the feelings of rejection and betrayal I suffered as an abandoned child. I was experiencing posttraumatic stress. The painful wounds of the new trauma unearthed the childhood memories that I'd buried. It was like my brain went back and located the hurt from the past, brought it to the present, and multiplied the emotional response. My pain was one of the consequences of my unfinished business from childhood and, if pain was an indicator of brokenness, I was shattered.

The pain I experienced, however, was disproportionate to the circumstances. I had grieved other losses in the past, but there was something distinctly different about the death of this friendship that left me raw and aching in ways I hadn't felt in years.

I was desperate to feel better, so I knew I was going to have to identify what I was feeling and process the emotions. To do that, I had to take a deeper look at what was really going on inside of me. I had a choice: either put a magnifying glass on my behavior and work to heal the root cause or deny my feelings and face the consequences of the unhealthy choices I would make because of them. I was starting to see that because I had avoided looking at the hurt of my past, I had unconsciously recreated it by repeating patterns of behavior that were wreaking havoc in my life.

When Mom left our family that spring day in 1972, I was changed. Not temporarily, but forever. When the very person who should have loved me the most abandoned me, my identity changed. I went from "I am loved unconditionally" to "I better be good so love stays." I responded to those life circumstances by doing what came naturally and what made sense to me. I did what I needed to do to gain back some of the power and control I'd lost. I came to believe that I needed to control the things I could because apparently, there was a lot I couldn't control. I created an environment around me that felt safe. I needed people, even though I couldn't trust them to provide the unconditional love I missed out on. My identity, although deeply wounded on the inside, still looked okay on the outside—I always made sure of that. I was never going to be unprepared again. I was not going to experience that kind of pain again.

19

I always did what I had to do to get my needs met. My need for unconditional love and support drove my behavior from the time my mom left through adulthood. I looked to people and depended on them to meet my needs. I was the perfect candidate for unhealthy dependency. My fear of abandonment and rejection caused me to choose friends that struggled with boundaries. Enmeshment meant I felt needed and was the center of their lives. Having healthy boundaries felt like I was unnecessary, and I was terrified of being unnecessary.

At this point in my life, I had worked to heal my emotions to a degree. I had even done some important forgiveness work around my mom's rejection. I had tried to live a better and healthier life and pass on what I had learned to others. I knew the pain of betrayal and rejection wasn't just a feeling; it was a belief in who I thought I was. At the heart of rejection for me was the belief that I could keep someone close if I was good enough, or kind enough, or just enough.

But I hadn't been enough to keep Ruth. It had only been a few weeks since our breakup, and I had a heavy heart. So, when Barry left for work on Monday morning, I resumed my place in front of the fire to spend some more time self-reflecting. I poured my second cup of coffee, grabbed a few books, a journal, and a pen, and sat down. As disheartened as I felt about my lost friendship, I knew time spent journaling was what I needed. I also knew the year was coming to an end, and I had some business to take care of before the calendar turned to the new year.

I was hurting emotionally and was struggling to do the things that I knew were good for me. I knew even though I didn't *feel* like doing the next right thing, that was exactly what I needed to do. After journaling for a bit, I decided to follow through with something I did every year in the fall: choose a word for the next year.

My word of the year had become a pretty serious deal to me. It was a tradition that started as a casual and fun exercise, but over the years, it had turned into something life-changing for me. Although I was feeling less than excited about choosing a word—or doing anything else positive for that matter—I had a feeling the word I chose for the coming year would be important. Each year I used my word to set goals and inspire me in every area of my life. I allowed my word to influence me and have a powerful effect on the direction my life took. I studied my word, focused on it, and became a student of it.

So, as I sat this November morning, I asked myself the question: *What do I need?* The answer was simple, yet complex. I needed to heal my adolescent years. I needed to create good-time experiences and heal those wounded places of my past. I needed to finish some business of my childhood and help that teenager heal her identity. I needed to discover what was influencing my current behavior and causing so much pain regarding my shattered friendship. As I thought that through, my word for the year rose up inside of me, and there was no denying it.

REDEEMED. To buy back; to regain possession of; to recover ownership; to make good; to fulfill.

Wasn't that exactly what I wanted to do? Make time good again? Redeem my adolescence? Heal the past? The definition of the word described what I was trying to accomplish that year, but what would that mean for me?

To buy back. What would it mean for me to buy back what I had lost? What had I lost? What would I need to "buy" for that little girl in the present day to replace what she had lost in the past? What would that cost me?

Regain possession of. How would I regain possession of what was taken away from me? How would I regain the truth of my identity? How would I come to know that I was enough, that I am enough?

To recover ownership. What did I need to own today that my past took from me? Where would I find it? How would I recover what I lost?

22

To make good. Could I really take those bad times and make them good? Was that possible? Could I experience time with truth and grace and make time good again?

To fulfill. Would I be able to realize and bring about what I needed the most: to know that I was loved unconditionally despite my mom abandoning me?

I wanted to experience the work of redemption in my life. I wanted to heal from my current pain, knowing it was in direct relationship to my past. I wanted to heal past wounds so I wouldn't repeat my dependency pattern again. I believed and was hopeful that I could redeem those years. I was optimistic because I knew I was personally responsible for the work that needed to take place in my life. I was functioning in unhealthy ways in my adulthood because of the wounds of my past, and it was time to change that. I was going to go back and heal those painful adolescent years that were still influencing my life. I was on a mission.

I thought about what I had read in *Changes That Heal* about redeeming time. Dr. Cloud said, "It's never too late to open up to those who love us and care about our development." Bennett had said that too. I could use current, healthy relationships to provide the nurturing I didn't receive as a child and the companionship I needed as a teenager. If I chose, I could recreate those experiences now and influence and develop the aspects of myself that were lost.

That's it. I am going to open up to those who love me and care about me. I am going to ask them to help me, even though that's difficult for me. I was pushed out of time as an adolescent and learned, because of what I had experienced, to take care of myself. It wasn't natural for me to ask for help, even from the people closest to me. I didn't trust people to follow through, so I typically just did it myself. I didn't lean on people who loved me in case they weren't there when I fell. It happened to me as a child with my mom, and it was happening to me again with a friend. Trusting people wasn't my strong suit.

I was a walking contradiction. I was dependent on others, but I didn't trust them. I needed people in my life to stay close to me and meet my needs, all while I continued to be fiercely independent. It was time for me to look at those unhealthy patterns and heal the root cause of that behavior. I knew I needed to nurture some new healthy relationships as well, and that was going to take courage. I had to be brave and trust people deeply if I wanted to heal completely.

I sat and prayed about it and asked God to show me some women who would be able to stand in the gap. Women who could give me not only time but love as well. Women who, despite my unhealthiness and dependency on others, would be safe for me. Women who would extend grace to me while still being strong enough to share truth. It didn't take long to come up with a list of four women who I believed would support me through this process. Each had overcome difficulties and had been transformed in their own life journeys. I had a feeling they could help lead me to where I needed to go.

I got up from my warm spot in front of the fire, went to the office, and sat down at the computer before I could talk myself out of my plan. I wrote my four friends a letter and emailed it, asking them to guide me through my year of redemption.

The letter described my word for the year and my plan to redeem my adolescence. I let my friends know I needed them to help me accomplish my redemption. I asked if they would individually spend a few mornings or afternoons with me in the coming year to share in some lost experiences. I wrote, "I hope to share some practical experiences that an adolescent needs and some emotional connections as well."

I hit send, closed my computer, and took a deep breath to soothe the rising anxiety. *What will they say? Will they reject me too?* There's something about being rejected by your mom that whispers, "You're not worthy! You're not worthy of their love, and you're surely not worthy of their time."

As I awaited their answers that afternoon, I distracted myself. I folded the laundry, took Bailey for a walk, and made dinner for Barry. By the end of the day, my fears proved to be unfounded. They all replied lovingly and seemed to be honored to help me. I still had a long way to go when it came to trusting, even safe people, and giving my heart away again. I believed God had supplied these women, so I started the process by trusting Him.

If I had waited to write that letter or to heal a bit more before I contacted my "redeeming ladies" as I fondly named them, I'm sure I would have talked myself out of the redeeming year ahead. I didn't come up with a hopeful plan for my redemption by waiting for the plan to come to me. I chose that morning to do the next right thing, and now I'd put into motion some new routines, inspiring experiences, and safe connections with four loving women.

Redeemed. A word that I hoped would not only change my year but my life.

4

The Bread of Life

C hange is inevitable, but growth is not. I had to be proactive in my approach to find emotional healing and growth. When January rolled around, I already had excuses as to why I couldn't make my year of redemption happen. I wasn't in a place emotionally to feel like spending the day with someone. I was down in the dumps, which was not typical for me around the new year. Usually I felt inspired and hopeful, but not this year. The loss of my friendship with Ruth continued to affect me deeply. I was struggling with anxiety and feeling depressed. The very things I needed, like connection with others and relationships in community, were what I tried to avoid. Isolation felt protective and safe, but isolation wasn't going to bring about healing. It would have been more comfortable for me to put off my redemption plan, but thanks to my redeeming ladies, it was happening whether I felt like it or not. My friend Nancy was the first redeeming lady on the calendar.

Nancy drove forty minutes across town and showed up at my house around ten in the morning with all the ingredients necessary to make her famous braided bread.

I heard the knock at the door and smiled as I opened it wide to welcome my friend.

"Thanks for being here, Nancy. This really means a lot to me."

Nancy's eyes twinkled. "I wouldn't want to be anywhere else today, hon." She gave me a quick hug and whispered, "This is going to be a great day." She stepped inside and walked to the kitchen island to set down her bag. "Your house is going to smell delicious by the time I leave here today."

I had met Nancy at The Healthy Weigh, the business I owned and operated. We fell into a close relationship shortly after she started working there. She wasn't old enough to be my mother, but she was as nurturing and loving to me as if I were one of her own. She was an obvious choice when I thought about who could help me redeem my adolescence.

The year I met Nancy, I had worked in the weight-loss industry for over twenty years. I started with the company when I was twenty-three years old. After nine years in the business, I bought a couple of locations when the owner of the company, which had locations nationwide, put them all up for sale. I had a choice: buy the business or close the doors and be out of a job. I stepped into being a business owner by default; it hadn't really been a goal of mine. The choice to buy the business, however, put me on a path of spending my life helping other people change theirs. It was a decision I never regretted.

My business concentrated primarily on physical weight loss, but I learned early on in my career that our external health is in direct relationship to our internal health. My professional focus over the years centered on emotional healing. As I studied and educated myself about healing the mind and body for the purpose of helping my clients, it influenced and helped me too.

I had highs and lows over the years at The Healthy Weigh, both financially and professionally. I held it together with the help of a line of credit and sheer determination to not fail. The motivation to appear successful was a driving force in my long-term achievement at work and, for that matter, in every area of my life. From the time my mom left our home, I learned to make things look good on the surface, and that "skill" helped me persevere in business, even through the hardest times. So much so, that I went without a paycheck throughout the years in order to cover my obligations. People wouldn't have known the difficulties the business was having because things looked good from the outside. I believed that if I looked like I achieved enough, somehow, I'd *be* enough. So, I just kept at it.

Nancy laid out the ingredients on the granite counter and pulled the recipe out of her bag while I turned on the oven. In my line of work, bread was an often-talked-about food group. I talked about it much more than I ate it, though, and I had never baked it. I loved that Nancy chose bread-making for our first redeeming day together. Baking bread takes time. I knew we were going to have to let it rest and rise, so we would have some real quality time together. That's just what I needed—uninterrupted time spent shoulder to shoulder with a loving woman.

I had given some thought in advance about how to approach my redeeming days. I knew I would need to allow myself to step back and experience those days from the perspective of a young girl. That's not easy to do when you're in your fifties and the parent of an adult child, but I knew it would be important if I wanted to heal those wounded places of my past. I'd encouraged my redeeming ladies to feel free to teach me, although I had been in relationships with them as equals for many years. At The Healthy Weigh I'd been Nancy's boss, but today I set our professional relationship aside and chose to be taught instead of teaching. I set my adult self aside and chose to be parented instead of parenting.

Nancy was one of the most gifted homemakers I'd ever met. I had referred to her over the years as Martha Stewart; in fact, she kind of resembled her. Nancy usually swept her soft, chin-length hair to the side and held it back with an ornate hair clip. Even on casual days, she dressed elegantly. She was a loving wife, mom, and grandmother, and had extraordinary skills when it came to the kitchen, the garden, and everything in her home. I respected her greatly and I was humbled, but somewhat insecure, about the time she would give to nurture me. Working together over the years with me in the lead role was a lot different than receiving the very personal gift of Nancy's time. I took a deep breath and tried to stay present to receive the love and attention she was there to give me.

With her warm and loving style, Nancy seemed to automatically take on the mother role. She patiently guided me through the steps of her time-tested braided bread recipe. I learned that baking bread is an art and a science. The first step was to understand the whole yeast thing. Nancy checked the water temperature on her wrist, but with my lack of experience, I opted for a thermometer. Once the yeast had "bloomed," I measured the rest of the ingredients, then mixed and kneaded. I kneaded that dough for fifteen minutes! I couldn't help but think while I kneaded that Nancy chose an activity that took time . . . lots of time.

"Nanc," I said, pausing my kneading for a minute, "I'm realizing that I don't have a memory of much time in the kitchen with my mom unless I was doing dishes. Our time together was never about creating things; it was practical and task-driven."

"I can imagine being one of eight children left little time for a one-on-one nurturing relationship with your mom."

"That's so true. When I look back on time spent with Mom, I had very few close encounters with her leading up to her departure. Maybe it was because she was unhappy with herself? Or maybe she had just run out of what she needed to be an engaged parent by the time she got to me."

Nancy stepped over and gave me a quick sideways hug. "I'm sorry, hon."

I went back to kneading. With Nancy, baking in the kitchen didn't feel like a task. It felt more like she really wanted to spend time with me and was enjoying it for herself as much as I was. My thirteen-year-old self needed to know I was important enough to spend time with. *You are worthy of Nancy's undivided time and attention,* I reminded myself. I chose to experience the day with my friend from a different perspective.

It was time to let the bread rise. "Do you have a tea towel?" Nancy asked.

I took a brand-new green-and-beige plaid cotton tea towel out of the drawer and placed it over the bowl of dough, then allowed time and warmth to do the rest. There was a fire in the fireplace just off the kitchen, so the room was warm, and the conditions were perfect for bread to rise and friends to catch up.

We sat down to the lunch I had prepared and talked about our plans for the year ahead. Nancy smiled. "I've been thinking about how we'll spend our time together this year, but I want to keep some things a secret so you have some surprises to look forward to."

"Hmmm, surprises. I've never been good about anticipating surprises. I wonder what that's about?" I said with a grin. I knew exactly what that was about. I didn't like the feeling of being out of control. I needed to know what was happening ahead of time and be assured that I wouldn't be caught off guard. *This year is going to stretch me. What have I done?*

Nancy stood to put our dishes in the sink. "Don't worry, I've got your back. You can count on me."

I wanted to believe that.

Nancy returned and reached into her bag, pulling out her Bible. "I brought something I thought you'd like to see." She flipped it open to show me the art journaling she'd been doing. *Journal* was her word for the year, and her Bible was being turned into a work of art, capturing Scripture with images using colored pencils. She was a talented artist, and her creation was something to behold. "Here's a page you'll want to see. It's perfect for today," Nancy said, flipping the delicate pages in her Bible to a chapter of John. Overlaying the entire sixth chapter was a drawing of a light-brown loaf of bread. She read, "Then Jesus declared, I am the bread of life. Whoever comes to me will never go hungry, and whoever believes in me will never go thirsty."

The smell of bread dough wafted through the air.

"You're right," I said. "That couldn't be more perfect for today." Nancy was making something beautiful based on her word for the year, and I hoped I was too.

It was time to lift the tea towel off the bread and, oh my, it had risen. It had risen indeed! I braided it (under close supervision), let it rise again for another thirty minutes, then put it in the oven. My house never smelled better. In fifty minutes, I pulled out the most beautiful, braided bread I had ever seen. It was the first braided bread I'd ever seen, but who's counting? It was slightly browned, with Nancy's secret seeds sprinkled over the top. It glistened because of the egg wash painted over the top.

"It's gorgeous. I can't believe I made this," I said.

Nancy smiled. "You did great. I just knew you'd love it. I am as thrilled as if I had shown my own daughter how to bake bread for the first time."

"Thanks, Nanc. I know how much you love your daughters, so that says a lot."

I took some pictures of our luscious loaves of bread

and a selfie or two of me and Nancy so I'd have a digital reminder. I was sure even without a picture I would always remember this experience. After spending most of the day with me, Nancy gathered up her things to go, leaving both loaves of bread with me. I gave her a hug and said goodbye. She looked back over her shoulder and said, "Until next time."

I closed the front door and started to weep. I cried because I felt love from Nancy when I didn't feel worthy of it. I allowed myself to be the center of someone's focus in a healthy way, but it felt uncomfortable. I wanted to believe and hope for the healing of my thirteen-year-old self, but I was having trouble connecting to her. Wiping my tears, I thought, *Is this decision to focus on healing the past really going to make a difference in my present?* I couldn't wrap my mind around how making time good and redeeming lost time from my past was going to change anything about today. How was focusing on the abandonment of my past going to change the pain I was feeling about the perceived abandonment in my present? Despite spending an entire day with a precious friend, I didn't feel much better. I didn't feel different.

I held on to Nancy's words, "until next time." I was going to have to trust the process and keep moving forward with my plan to redeem lost time and make it good. I had to trust that present experiences would help heal and redeem the past. I had to keep trying.

After I cleaned up the kitchen, I sat down and wrote an email to my four redeeming ladies. I wanted all four of them to share in the entire experience that year. I decided to write them each month as soon as the redeeming day was over, when my feelings were still tangible and my emotions were high. I wanted to capture how I was feeling, not only so they could share in my journey of healing, but so I would have a reminder of all the changes that were happening to me. I wept while I wrote, then pushed send. One redeeming day down, eleven to go. Until next time.

5

It's a Sacred Journey

I tossed and turned Wednesday night. The thought of meeting a counselor and spilling my guts the following day kept me awake until the early hours of the morning. I knew I needed a safe place to tell my story, but there was a big part of me afraid to share it. I had spent many years of my life showing the world a certain side of me for a reason. I believed if I gave enough of myself, others wouldn't leave me. Entering into a counseling scenario meant I was going to need to get honest about those beliefs. Honesty felt super vulnerable. Even though I hadn't met Suzy yet, I already cared about what she would think about me. If I told her the truth, would she still like me? If I shared my fears, would she consider me weak? I wanted everyone to like me, and most people who knew me considered me to be a tower of strength. I also knew once I shared my fears and struggles, there was no going back.

I had been to counselors in the past and had worked through various issues. The forgiveness work I had done surrounding my mom was the catalyst for my reconciliation with her. I'd forgiven Mom for leaving me on the curb and choosing another man over our family, for not engaging with me during my teenage years, and so much more. All that important work on my end had created new opportunities for my mom and me to connect in my adult years. For that I was so grateful.

The discovery I was on now, so many years later, was not so much about my relationship with my mom as it was my relationship with myself. I could continue to blame my abandonment for my unhealthy choices and dependency on others, or I could find a safe place to peel back another layer and get to the issues beneath the surface. I was hoping and praying I was about to find a secure place for deeper self-discovery.

I had a fun and creative plan to redeem my adolescence with my redeeming ladies, but I knew the year couldn't be only about recreating childhood experiences. Abandonment, rejection, and betrayal were part of my story, and the roots ran deep. I was living my fifty-seventh year of life but still responding from the wounds of an abandoned child. My thirteen-year-old self was contaminating my adult life. I knew I was going to have to examine those roots and understand more about myself.

Suzy was a therapist who had been referred to me by a leader at a women's prayer event I'd attended a few weeks earlier. I wasn't a stranger to women's events at church. In fact, I'd been the organizer of many of them over my lifetime. But I'd gone to this one—at a church I wasn't a member of, where I didn't know anyone—to prevent myself from stepping into a helper role, the role I was used to playing in so many areas of my life. I attended the event hoping to receive some wise mentoring, but, instead, I was the elder in a group of mostly young women. Sweet as they were, I didn't feel they could speak to my situation. At the end of the night, our group facilitator provided a resource sheet. At the top of the page was a list of counselors. There was a little heart by Suzy's name and a handwritten note, "She's awesome."

When I scheduled the appointment with Suzy, I hadn't paid much attention to her address. Even though I knew it was in Portland, I wasn't aware of just how long a drive it would be. I pulled into the parking lot of her office about forty-five minutes after leaving home. With a queasy stomach and shaky hands, I rang the little doorbell outside her office door. A few minutes later a woman, who seemed about five or so years older than me with light-brown hair and a warm smile, opened the door.

"Letha?"

I nodded.

"I'm Suzy, so nice to meet you. I'll have you wait for a few minutes; I'm just finishing up with another appointment."

I followed her to an adjoining room, where I sat and waited for her to come and retrieve me. It was just a few minutes, but it felt longer. Part of me thought, *I still have time to bolt.* I had already convinced myself that it was too long a drive to make on any kind of regular basis. About then, she cracked open the door and said, "I'm ready for you." I wondered if she was.

I followed her into her office. It was bigger than I thought it would be. The windows on two sides let in light that brightened the room. There was a long, beige couch with floral pillows, two light-blue side chairs, end tables with pretty lamps, and a bookshelf with a ton of books. Suzy sat in a wingback chair across from the couch. She invited me to sit where I felt comfortable. I chose the couch.

She said, "Letha, you shared a bit about what's been going on with you over email. Tell me more."

I spent the next thirty minutes or so telling her about my current situation with the loss of my longtime friend and filling her in about my family of origin. She took lots of notes as I talked, looking up to smile or ask another question.

"I'm here because the depth of pain I'm currently feeling is disproportionate to the story I'm living," I finally told her.

Suzy stopped writing, looked up, and with a twinkle in her eyes said, "Oh, Letha, there's nothing disproportionate about the pain you're feeling."

That's when I started to cry. She leaned forward and handed me the box of Kleenex that sat on the coffee table between us.

"Letha, you might not have had the tools, support, or safety you needed to acknowledge and accept the pain of your past. And that's okay because you're safe now. You can begin to process the feelings you've denied for a long time—not to blame, but to heal yourself for a better life in the future. Those painful experiences in your past haven't gone anywhere. They will keep coming up for you until they get your attention. I feel like that's where you are now . . . and that's a really good thing. Understanding your story is the single most important thing you can do for your brain, your heart, and your body to heal from the wounds of living in a broken world."

Relief swept over me that maybe I had found a place where I could share my story and be heard. And maybe I'd found a place where I could show weakness and not be judged. I glanced out the window for a moment. *I think grace and truth are going to collide in this office.*

41

We talked for a few more minutes. Suzy said, "Letha, if you feel like you want to pursue healing here with my support, I'll set up another appointment with you and give you a bit of homework."

"I'd like that." And I meant it. I felt a sense of optimism that I hadn't felt in months.

Suzy went to her file cabinet and pulled out a few pieces of paper. She also stopped at her bookshelf and grabbed a book. She handed the sheets of paper to me and explained them a bit. The header said "Life Impact Worksheet." In filling it out, I was to start with my earliest memories. Memories, Suzy said, that were negative or hurtful to me. She explained that starting from the beginning would give me a systematic way to move through my life. "The beginning of one's life matters the most, Letha. Spend some time on this and bring it back to your next appointment. We'll start from the beginning." Then she handed me a book, *Safe People,* by Dr. Henry Cloud.[3] I smiled at the familiar name of the author who had inspired my redemption year in the first place. She said, "If you have time this week, I'd love you to start reading this book. *Safe People* will give you the tools you need to recognize what makes people relationally safe and to form positive relationships in the future."

I briefly told her about my redeeming ladies and the plan I had set up for my year of redemption. She seemed

42

pleased to hear about the safe people I already had put in place in my life to move through this time of healing.

"Letha, I've never heard of anyone doing that before. You've come up with a practical but deeply personal way to take back some of those lost experiences. You are going to change some old narratives with some new actions. I really love the sound of that. I look forward to seeing you next week and hearing more about it. Between the work you and I will do together and the plan you've made with your redeeming ladies, you're going to be okay."

I walked out of her office feeling better and much more hopeful than when I entered, but also a little apprehensive about what my homework would bring up for me. I had just committed to another appointment and was ready to look at some experiences I had been denying for a lifetime. I found the forty-five-minute drive home was the perfect amount of time to process what I'd just learned and think about what would come next.

That week, I waited until I knew I had time to focus and sit awhile to tackle my homework. I grabbed a blanket to keep warm, got comfortable out on my back deck, and started in. It was my job to *collect* the dots before I could *connect* the dots. I said a little prayer that memories would come to me, and boy did they. I hadn't thought about some of those people or experiences in, well, maybe forever. I cataloged the story of being left on the curb that spring day when I was thirteen, but that wasn't the only time I'd been left on the curb.

When I was six years old, we attended a church some thirty miles or so from our home. My dad drove a Sunday school bus and picked up kids all along the route from our house to the church. Dad would go pick up the bus on Saturday night, leave his car at the church, and park the bus in front of our house so we could leave from home on Sunday morning. Most of us kids (there were six of us left at home by then) rode the bus with him. My oldest brother, Dougie, would sit up in the seat behind Dad, but the rest of us sat in the very back, waiting for the big bump over the railroad tracks. It felt like we bounced ten feet in the air. Things feel big when you're six years old. Mom would drive her car and meet us at church. Dad left the bus at the church on Sundays and took his car home until the next weekend, when he'd do it again.

That Sunday, I didn't end up in either car for the long ride home. Church was out, people were leaving, and suddenly I realized I didn't see any of my family. I frantically ran to the front parking lot of the church and then to the back parking lot. Neither Mom's nor Dad's car was there. I imagine they both thought the other one had me, but that was of no consequence to me. I was left behind.

I was too shy to tell anyone still left in the building, so I anxiously made my way out to the front of the church and sat down on the curb, thinking that's where they'd come back to find me. I sat next to the road in my Sunday dress with my blond pixie haircut and waited. No one came. When cars drove by, I'd lower my head to prevent eye contact so I wouldn't have to explain why I was there. As the last car was leaving the parking lot, it slowed to a stop and a man rolled down his window. It was our pastor.

"Letha?"

I looked up with tears in my eyes. "Yes?"

"What are you doing here?" he asked tenderly.

I told him I was waiting for my mom or dad to come get me.

"Oh, Letha," he said, "let's go give them a call." He parked his car, and he and his wife took me into the church with them. They called my mom and dad, who still hadn't realized I wasn't home. They were horrified. Mom drove back as quickly as she could to get me. The pastor and his wife waited with me until she arrived, which was about forty minutes later. After I got in the car, Mom drove about a block away then turned to me and angrily said, "Where were you? Why weren't you in the car? What were you thinking anyway?"

I had thought she was going to apologize for forgetting me. Instead, I was bad and in trouble. I answered sheepishly, "I don't know."

We didn't speak the rest of the way home.

As I filled out the worksheet, I began to recognize my healing was going to be about connecting the dots between childhood wounds and the emotional responses in my adult life. I was starting to see how the beliefs I had about myself and others came out of those life experiences. Recognizing and acknowledging them was an important step to understanding myself as an adult. However, the next step would be the important one—healing those wounded places so I could live my healthiest emotional life as an adult.

As I filled out my life impact worksheet, I included any incident that I could remember; good or bad. I worked to recollect all the significant events that played a role in my life—events that were like doorways. Once I experienced them, I never walked back through that doorway again— the events that changed my life forever. The goal of my homework was to identify why I believed what I believed. Giving my life some order (in terms of chronology) helped me see when:

- I began to feel as though I had to be perfect or perform

- I began to feel like I had to give everything of myself so others wouldn't leave me
- I felt like I wasn't enough
- I quit trusting people
- I closed my heart
- I looked to others to get my needs met
- I quit using my voice
- I allowed myself to be controlled
- I controlled things outside of myself to feel in-control.

Once I was done with my life impact sheet, I took those events and categorized them on another worksheet Suzy had given me. On this second sheet, I was to identify the source of my pain related to these events and put them in one of three columns: shame, fear, or control. Almost every experience I identified ended up in the shame column. Abandonment, poverty, feeling unwanted and neglected . . . all ended up in the shame column. I was shocked. Never in my life had I attached that word to myself. Never. Shame doesn't say I made a mistake, it says I *am* a mistake. Shame says I am flawed, I am bad, and I am defective. This realization was going to help me tremendously with my healing and growth. Honesty, although painful, was a giant step toward my healing.

Sitting on my deck that afternoon, I saw why I had

created a persona around me. I saw why I reached outside of myself to get my needs met and why I strived so hard to make life look good. I was born complete and happy, and then things happened in my life to change that. I believed, whether it was true or not, something was wrong with me, so I created a false self to cover my shame.

I took those worksheets back to Suzy the following week and we started at the top, or should I say, the beginning. We began to unpack each story tenderly. Suzy said it was important for me to unfold the memories slowly enough to address them and heal them. I learned to stay emotionally present as I told her my stories with as many details as I could remember.

When I was preparing to leave her office that day, having wept my way through the hour, Suzy said, "Letha Janelle (I soon learned that she used my middle name when she was about to say something really important), I'm so honored to go on this sacred journey with you. Thank you for allowing me to be part of it."

Sacred. She called my journey sacred. I thought about that all the way home, and it was the boost I needed that day. Sacred meant this painful time I was experiencing was holy and connected to God. My healing, despite how hard it felt, was blessed. I was on a difficult and painful journey to redeem lost time and, as emotional as it was, it felt a little better that day knowing it was sacred.

6

Retail Therapy

I had gone months without talking to Ruth. That was painful for me, considering we used to talk almost daily. Experiencing that emptiness while choosing to work through the issues of my childhood was depressing. Even though it was only a few months into the year, there were days I thought, *I should be feeling better than this by now.* I was slowly accepting that there was no timeline to bouncing back. I was learning to accept where I was each day and process those feelings. It seemed the less I tried to feel better, the better I felt. But I understood that simply letting time pass was not the key to healing my emotions. Accepting things as they were, while I actively took part in my redeeming process, was crucial for my continued healing. I was learning to be balanced in my approach, and balance didn't come easy for me.

Grieving my current loss and healing from my painful past wasn't as systematic as I wished. It wasn't like climbing the rungs of a ladder one at a time and going straight to the top. I would climb four steps up out of my dark hole and see a little light, then all of a sudden, I'd find myself down at the bottom rung again in the dark, thinking, *How'd I get here?* I was coming to understand this way of processing my pain as normal and healthy.

The day I met up with Judy, I was feeling better. We were going to do a simple mom/daughter activity: shopping and lunch. Shopping was one of the experiences I had missed out on. I didn't have any fun memories of a shopping day with Mom. I didn't learn the ins and outs of shopping for groceries or clothing as a teenager. I joked for years that I had a shopping disorder: I would spend money on food and have nothing to eat and spend money on clothing and have nothing to wear. I realized it wasn't so much a disorder, but a lack of experience.

Judy texted and recommended we meet at the Jantzen Beach shopping center. I couldn't believe she had suggested that location. How could she have known? Jantzen Beach shopping center evoked deep painful memories for me.

It was 1973. My older sister Vickie was living in a little apartment not far from our house. On Saturdays she would come pick me up and we would go do something fun together. Vickie and I were four years apart in age. We had shared a bedroom growing up with our twin beds on either side of the room. We had those groovy bedspreads you might have seen on the *Brady Bunch* with big, bright colorful daisies. It was mostly a good thing sharing a bedroom with my older sister. We did life together. We went on a lot of walks, laughed and talked at night in our room, and even shared our babysitting earnings to finance excursions to the neighborhood market for donuts and cherry Coke. I missed her, even though she lived just down the street.

Vickie had moved out before Mom left. She was eighteen and already on her own. When you grow up in a big family, you don't have much privacy and very little time to yourself. We shared the one bathroom in our home with the rest of the family. Vickie was the oldest daughter at home before she got her apartment, and that meant she shouldered more of the responsibility. She was excited to get out on her own and start her life away from home.

That Saturday, we were going shopping and planned to visit our mom at work. She worked at Montgomery Ward in the women's clothing department and was always there on Saturdays. Mom had been out of our house and living with her boyfriend for about six months by this time. We didn't see or hear much from her. If we were going to see her, we had to go to where she was. Life hadn't gotten easier for me, but it was becoming more normal.

Vickie picked me up in her 1963 baby-blue Ford Futura, and we drove over the interstate bridge to Jantzen Beach Mall. "How was your week?" Vickie asked. She was always so good at checking in with me.

"It was okay." I didn't have the ability to express what I was really feeling those days. "I'll be better after we see Mom." I hadn't eaten that morning and my stomach rumbled. I always felt a little nervous when we'd go to see Mom at work. *Would she have time for us? Would she even have anything to say? Would I have anything to say?* She didn't know how I spent my days, who I was hanging out with, or how things were going at our house.

Vickie pulled into the parking lot and parked the car close to the store entrance. We stopped at the perfume counter to spray on a sample before we went to see Mom. I spritzed a shot of Love's Baby Soft on my wrists, and Vickie chose Charlie. We strolled over to the women's department but didn't see Mom at the checkout counter. I asked the other three ladies working there, "Is Letha here?"

The ladies looked at each other uncomfortably, and one of them said, "No, she's not here today," with a flash of a smile, avoiding our gaze.

Vickie asked cheerfully, "Oh, well, when is she on the schedule again?"

Another one of the ladies stepped forward with a

flushed face, and said with a voice a little louder than a whisper, "Letha moved to Texas."

I covered my face with my hands and backed away from the counter without responding. I didn't have the words to speak or the courage to even look at my sister. I glanced around for a place to run and hide. I darted into a round rack of clothing hoping to become invisible. Panic enveloped me as I pressed into the folds of clothes. I bent over and tried to make myself small. I desperately held on to the base of the clothing rack, not knowing how I was going to get back up. Beads of sweat dripped down my face and my stomach started lurching. My mind couldn't process what was happening. Mom had moved to Texas, and she didn't tell us. She'd left again. Abandoned us again, betrayed us again. The feelings I had experienced six months earlier when Mom left compounded. I let out an uncontrolled moan and then pressed my palm over my lips to keep myself from sobbing.

I stayed where I was until I regained my composure, coming out of my hiding place to leave the store. Vickie and I walked out to the car without looking at each other. We had never been taught how to identify our feelings, so we lacked the skills to share them with each other. We shared our childhoods and our bedroom for most of our lives but still didn't have the ability to comfort or care for each other at that moment. I cried quietly all the way home and rolled down the window for some fresh air. The thought came over me as we drove back over the bridge that we were going to have to tell Dad and the boys. I rubbed my hands up and down my pants until I warmed up. The truth was catching up with me. My mom had not only left, but she had moved across the country without warning, without saying goodbye. It was now my responsibility to deliver the news to my already-hurting dad and brothers. *How would I say it? What would Dad do? How would my brothers respond?* I was doing business as an adult, not a thirteen-year-old.

Forty-four years later, driving over the interstate bridge to meet Judy at Jantzen Beach, the pain was still present. I shook my head as I drove, believing that God was in this redemption thing with me for sure. I was literally going back to that painful place to redeem my adolescence with a loving woman who would be there when I arrived.

I pulled into the parking lot right next to Judy. We got out of our cars and hugged. Judy looked put together in her bold black-and-yellow ensemble. From her chic hairstyle to her hip outfit, she was all the rage. In her seventies, Judy could inspire even the youngest fashionista. She inspired me. I smiled when we embraced and said, "Remind me to tell you a story about Jantzen Beach shopping center when we go to lunch; you're not going to believe it."

We were the first ones in the store. Judy was a bargain

shopper. I watched and learned. She had a list, of course, of things she needed to complete an outfit she already owned. Maybe that's where I had always gone wrong. I had ten incomplete outfits at home. We started at the back of the store because, as she said, "That's where the real bargains are," and then worked our way to the front. As we browsed the racks, she said, "Letha, always ask, 'Would this item go with at least three to five things I already own?' If the answer is no, put it back." And even though most shopping experts would say to avoid trends, that was *not* one of Judy's rules. She was one of the most fashion-forward women I knew. I loved that about her.

We took our finds back to the dressing room and parked ourselves across the aisle from each other so we could give the red or green light. We laughed, complimented each other, and were honest too. I tried on one top that I thought looked really great on me. When I came out of the dressing room to show Judy, she said, "That's not the best color on you." I smiled. It was probably just like it would have been had I shopped with my mom. And that's just what I needed. To buy back and regain possession of an experience I'd missed.

We made some purchases from a couple of different stores, then headed to lunch. We drove a mile down the road to the Island Café and were seated right next to the water. The Columbia River sparkled like diamonds in the warm sunshine. We enjoyed watching the kayakers and the ducks float on the water while we drank our iced tea and ordered our lunch.

Love and loss were the focus of our conversation at lunch. Judy had recently lost her husband and my friend, Ed. She was doing grief well, as grief goes. Her heart was being enlarged by the loss of her husband of over fifty years, even as she felt the deep sadness of his absence. The choices she was making to remember him, the love she was receiving from family and friends, and the care she was taking of herself were healing her and helping her find a new normal. I shared about my progress in grieving and redeeming—my efforts to create a new normal.

"You said you had a story to share," she reminded me. I briefly told her the story of the pain I had experienced at Jantzen Beach so many years ago.

"I'm so sorry, I didn't know. I wish I had chosen somewhere that didn't trigger bad memories for you." She paused, then smiled. "Wow, Letha, this day was really about redemption, wasn't it?" All I could do, because of the lump in my throat, was nod my head in agreement.

This day was one where we each accepted where we were on our own journeys and recognized that spending time together was an important piece of healing for both of us. That painful day at Montgomery Ward had never been healed, or for that matter, talked about again. I had thought those memories could live in the past, but I realized what's buried alive never dies. Healing had to go back to the original injury for me for the "weed to be pulled out by the root." I could have mowed over those dandelions for a lifetime and never gotten rid of them. Dandelions have roots that go deep into the soil, and, if you snap the root while trying to pull out the weed from your garden, it makes matters worse: the dandelion will only grow back in full force. I knew if I didn't go deep enough to take care of my painful memories for good, I'd deal with them for a lifetime. I would feel the effects of whatever was unresolved in my life for the rest of my life. I would either medicate the old injury, act out, or spend my life in denial and disconnected from the truth about myself.

I'm not sure if it was the retail therapy, having a meal on the waterfront in the sunshine, or sharing the stories of love and loss with a dear friend, but I was feeling a bit more cheerful on my drive home. That day and the week following, as I continued the healing work of redemption, I played that scene over in my mind and heart. I allowed myself to feel the feelings of that specific day and forgive Mom once again. I realized that working through painful episodes was a way of dealing with the trauma that had obviously lived with me for years. I was getting to the root of the feelings that had been smashed down and buried deep all those years ago. I was convinced, more than ever, that to be free and live joyfully, I needed to go back to go forward. As I pulled the weeds of my past, the garden of my heart began to change. New flowers bloomed where painful memories used to be buried.

Montgomery Ward was remodeled and turned into a Target store years after my mom worked there. The old Ward's escalators remained. When I take the Target escalator down now, it stops right in front of the women's department. I can almost smell Love's Baby Soft perfume and see that fearful fourteen-year-old girl peek out of the clothes rack. But now, instead of feeling shame and sorrow, I smile at the memory of my time with Judy, friendship, and belonging.

7

Secret Family Recipe

"Letha, you're here!" Karen greeted me at her front door with a warm hug. "I've been so looking forward to this day."

I noticed a big pile of shoes inside the door as I walked in, so I slipped mine off and added them to the heap.

Karen ushered me into her beautiful kitchen. The warm wood cabinets and dark stone countertops felt so inviting. Leather swivel bar stools lined an island big enough to seat six. I imagined her kids and grandkids sitting there as Karen prepared meals for her family. There was no doubt this room was the gathering place of her home. She had a candle lit and soft music playing. Her black pants and crisp white blouse looked perfect with her soft blond hair and the black apron she was wearing. She handed me an apron just like hers, and I slipped it over my head. Karen said, "Now, you know, I always keep two things in my apron pockets. A tube of lipstick and my cell phone."

"Well, hold on then." I went back to the entryway, grabbed both out of my purse, and slipped them into my apron pockets.

"Now we're ready," Karen said with a smile. "Let's get started. I have so many things I want to show you today." She walked over and picked up a piece of paper next to her sink. "I made a list of the things we're going to make today. I chose some favorite recipes to share with you. My girls and I make these all the time. I thought you'd love them too."

I had chosen Karen to be one of my redeeming ladies because her life represented the very thing I needed: redemption. She lived joyfully and courageously, even though she had experienced tragedy and deep pain in her life. She took care of herself, her family, and others with great passion. There was nothing she didn't do or wouldn't try. I had never met anyone quite like her, and her life's resumé inspired me. She had a full and busy life, but today she was taking time out of her schedule to spend it with me.

The idea that my redeeming ladies would take a full day out of their lives to spend time with me was one of the acts of love that were helping to heal my feelings of rejection. I couldn't remember spending one full day alone with my mom. Even when she was home, there was always a herd to care for. Mom was distracted because of her own unmet needs, and she wasn't attuned to mine. I learned, from the very beginning of my life, that I was just one of the pack. Being raised in a large family meant I never had individualized attention. The undivided attention my redeeming ladies gave me each month was not only kind but healing.

Asking them to spend time with me contradicted the belief system I'd been operating under for years, which said, "I'm not important enough to spend time with." My beliefs were so ingrained and unconscious that I hadn't become aware of their impact on my emotions and behaviors until now. Change was good, but it felt awkward. I was afraid of those awkward feelings until the need to change became greater than my need for comfort. My time with Nancy had helped me to begin addressing this insecurity, but I still felt uncomfortable.

Karen and I started with lasagna. Not just any lasagna—it was a secret Italian family recipe. Minutes after we got going, I said, "Could I have paper and a pencil so I can write down all you're teaching me?" She grabbed it for me. I wrote at the top of the page, *Karen's Kitchen Facts*. I didn't want to forget a thing she was casually mentioning as we worked together. Karen and I were experiencing a role reversal. Like Nancy, she had worked for me at The Healthy Weigh for years and was used to following my lead. Now, I was following hers.

"Karen, I hope this year you will feel comfortable going from mentee to mentor. I'm in need of some mothering, and I know it's not the relationship we're used to. This year, I really need you to think of me like one of your girls."

She timidly said, "Okay. It feels kind of funny for me, and I'm sure you must know all these kitchen basics, but I'll keep teaching if you say so."

She wouldn't have known just how little time I'd spent in the kitchen with my mom. The things that Karen was showing me that day might have seemed basic to her, but for me, they were the first time I'd heard about them.

My list of *Karen's Kitchen Facts* included:

- There's such a thing as oven-ready lasagna noodles
- Tomatoes eat through foil, so it's best to put parchment paper over the tomato dish first, then cover it with foil when baking
- Empty coffee creamer containers are great for making dressings-to-go or sharing with a friend
- You can make roux ahead of time and keep it in the fridge to use later (I didn't even know what roux was before my redeeming day with Karen)
- Keep a sink full of hot soapy water with a capful of bleach to clean up and sanitize the area while you're working (the dollar store sells small bottles of bleach to use and store under the kitchen sink)

Karen and I made lasagna, black bean enchiladas, skillet bread, and roux, and we even seasoned the new cast iron skillets I'd brought with me. Every yummy recipe was made to freeze, give away, or enjoy. I was working on layering the lasagna noodles when she looked over from across the kitchen and said, "Good job. That looks perfect. Now let's preheat the oven." Her words brought a sudden memory to mind. I told Karen about a time when I hadn't done such a perfect job in the kitchen.

I was fourteen years old and the woman of the house. Dad was working as a plumber, and my brothers were busy being teenage boys. I did my best to keep the house clean, do the laundry, and, on occasion, make a warm meal for my dad. We had slipped very easily into a routine of making frozen pizzas (usually Totinos because they went on sale), mac & cheese from a box, or sandwiches for most dinners. But this night was different. I wanted my dad to come home to a warm dinner after a cold day working outside, so I was making baked chicken with potatoes. I cut up a whole chicken and then prepared it using Shake 'n Bake seasoning. I laid each piece on a baking sheet with some seasoned potatoes. I glided around the kitchen, thinking of Dad walking in to find a warm meal. I put the dinner in the oven and set the timer. It'd be ready just about the time he got home from work.

When he walked in, I proudly said, "Dad, I made Shake 'n Bake chicken for dinner." About then, the timer went off and I went to the oven to pull it out. Problem was, I hadn't turned on the oven. With a heavy sigh, I sagged against the wall. My voiced dropped. "Oh, Dad, I didn't turn on the oven. That was stupid of me." As upset as I was, I still expected him to tell me that it was okay and we could bake it together. But he didn't say that.

"Lee Lee," he said with a shake of his head, "how could you have done that? Why didn't you notice it wasn't baking? How long is it going to take now?"

I was so disappointed in myself that he couldn't have made me feel worse. I had wanted so badly to create good, warm feelings in our house for my dad, but I failed.

Looking back, of course, I saw my dad in a different light. He was hungry, he was cold, and he was a broken man. His reaction wasn't about uncooked chicken, it was about his pain. I was a young girl, already trying to please people in pain. My identity was slowly forming. *If I'm good enough, the people around me will be happy. If I'm bad and make mistakes, the people closest to me will be unhappy and disappointed.*

I hadn't thought of that story for years until that moment in Karen's kitchen. Painful stories hit me at the most unexpected times. I was learning from Suzy that when I retold a sad story of my adolescence, the more specifics I remembered and shared, the deeper the healing was. I could almost smell the chicken that ended up coming out of the oven one hour late over forty-five years ago.

After we slipped the lasagna into the preheated oven, I looked in Karen's pantry (even my pantry needed redemption), saw what she kept under her kitchen sink, and asked her all kinds of questions about the favorite foods she prepared for her family. At one point in the afternoon, I texted Barry with a list of all we'd done, and he texted back, "Better than Sur La Table," referring to a Portland retail shop with terrific cooking classes. He was right . . . it was.

Karen was so sweet and patient with me all day, and a couple of times I teared up just experiencing her love. When I asked her how much I owed for all the ingredients, she said, "Nothing. That's what moms do." I had to choose to allow her to do that for me. It wasn't my normal response to receive from someone. I was much better at giving so I could control what happened to me. Receiving from someone meant opening myself up to get hurt all over again.

We loaded up my car late that afternoon with wonderful food and my seasoned skillets. "Thank you, Karen, for everything." I hugged her tight and held on for a bit.

"Oh, Letha, it was all my pleasure."

I took a couple of deep breaths as I started my drive home. I was feeling the warm emotions of being cared for so deeply, but at the same time recognizing just how much I'd missed growing up. Although I knew I was buying back time and making it good again, it was still sad for me. I wished time had just been good from the start. I knew if my mom had loved me differently, things would be different now. But there was no changing the past, there were only decisions to continue to make to change my future. I wanted to keep making them.

I arrived home and emailed my letter of reflection to my redeeming ladies while I was still feeling all the feelings of the day. Then I put the secret-Italian-family-recipe lasagna out on the table for Barry when he got home from work. My home felt warm on a cold night, and thanks to Karen and a preheated oven, dinner was ready right on time.

8

Superhero

I was connecting the dots from my childhood to my present-day life every week between my counseling appointments with Suzy. She had a knack for asking just the right questions to help my heart, mind, and body engage in stories from my past, stories that held big feelings for me. I realized that I had avoided a lot of memories because they didn't make me feel good. Suzy explained that lingering in a story and remembering details was required to grow and heal. I had a spirit of optimism that got in the way of my healing at times. The positive attitude I showed the world kept me in denial about some of the things in my past that I needed to heal and let go of. It was a good thing I didn't need to prove anything to Suzy or be a certain way with her. I could tell her anything and be completely honest about my feelings. But honesty was hard for me, especially in the areas where I had been in denial about myself and my relationships. The more real I got with myself, the greater my understanding was about where I came from and what my upbringing had to do with how I was feeling currently.

The healing work got extra hard one week when Suzy pulled another book off the shelf for me to take home and read—*Codependent No More* by Melodie Beattie.[4] Codependency was a title I had assigned to others and understood to a degree, but now I was looking in the mirror and seeing where it was true of me. People-pleasing, fear of abandonment, and wanting to feel in control were all a part of what I was feeling . . . and what I was healing. I was learning that I developed these traits early in my childhood, not only because of my physical abandonment, but also as a result of our family dynamics.

Suzy asked me that Tuesday afternoon if I could remember a specific story about taking care of my brothers after Mom left. It only took me seconds to put myself right back in our house on West 29th Street. I was fifteen years old. I told Suzy the whole story.

Mom was gone, and I believed that I had to take on the task of parenting my brothers and caring for my dad. When I was pushed out of time as an adolescent, I shifted into my new adult role and took it seriously. The problem was, my brothers didn't want to be parented by me. We were the last three born in our family and we were only seventeen months apart. It made for some fun when we were in school because we filled a spot in each grade level, but it wasn't so fun when I tried to mother them.

My older brother Joey was driving, so he wasn't home as much for me to boss around, but Mark and I were together all the time. Sometimes we had fun; other times we clashed. I tried to tell him what to do, and that didn't always sit well with him.

Joey had the basement bedroom, and Mark had moved from the basement to the room across the hall from me sometime after Vickie moved out. He was a typical teenage boy and didn't care how his room looked or smelled. Vickie had taken all the bedroom furniture with her, but that didn't bother Mark. He pulled out a sleeping bag and crashed on the floor. His bedding was on the floor, his clothes were on the floor, and, in fact, everything he owned was on the floor. I was about to do something about that.

Mark was going camping with a friend and his family for the weekend. I took that as an opportunity to transform his room and create a better space for him. He left early Saturday morning, and I got started.

First, I had to fumigate the room. I took everything out: the dirty clothes, the dirty dishes, and the dirty sleeping bag. I vacuumed the patchwork carpet and wiped down the walls. Then I started gathering things from all parts of the house to make a proper bedroom for my little brother. I went down to the basement and dragged a twin bed frame and mattress up two flights of stairs. I'm not even sure how I did that alone, but I was determined to make his life better and it gave me superhero strength. I found clean sheets and bedding, a side table, and a funky little hand-painted lamp. I repurposed some old blacklight posters the boys had previously used in their room downstairs and hung them on the wall. I washed, dried, and hung his clothes in the bedroom closet and moved a little dresser from my room to his for the rest of his things. It was adorable! I finished all of this on Saturday night and had to wait until Sunday afternoon to see his reaction. I barely slept.

Mark arrived home Sunday, tired and grimy from his camping trip. I couldn't even wait for him to get cleaned up to show him his surprise. He followed me up the stairs. I pushed the bedroom door open and let him go in first. He walked in, looked around, and started to cry. He turned around, hugged me, and whispered, "Thank you, Letha. This is unbelievable. I can't believe you did this for me." I cried too. I got the reaction I was hoping for. I showed him his closet and all his clean clothes and then left him to hang out in his new room alone. He was lying on his bed when I walked out. I had a lightness in my chest, and warmth spread through my entire body.

It had been a year since Mom left, and I had taken on the role of rescuer. Mark was eleven years old when she left. He needed rescuing, and I longed to be needed. It gave me a strong sense of self and helped bridge the gap in our home where love was missing. I needed to care for Mark, possibly more than he needed. This self-imposed assignment I gave myself carried awesome power for me. It truly was as though I had a superhero's cape on when I stepped in to help my brothers or my dad. It became the way I felt connected and loved.

One night a few weeks after the bedroom makeover, Dad and Mark were downstairs in the family room watching TV. I was upstairs in my room, hanging out. I walked across the hall to look into Mark's room. I wanted to experience the warm feelings again of how it felt to create a good space for him. I couldn't believe what I saw when the door swung open. Clothes covered the carpet, dirty dishes littered every surface, the bedding drooped off the backside of the bed, and the room smelled like a teenage boy again. I snapped.

I stomped down the stairs and stormed into the family room. I shouted, "Mark, get upstairs right now and clean your room! I can't believe how bad your room looks, and after all I did for you. Go do it right now!"

Dad chimed in calmly, using Mark's nickname. "Little Dude, do what your sister wants. Get on up there and clean your room." Mark gave me a dirty look, stormed out of the room, and trudged up the stairs. I felt some satisfaction that my dad was supporting my request, making Mark clean his room. I sat down with a sigh on the couch next to Dad and watched whatever he was watching on TV, mostly to stay out of Mark's way. He showed back up in the family room in fewer than ten minutes.

I looked up. "That was fast."

He said, "I work fast, and it wasn't that dirty."

I couldn't help myself. I pretended I was just going back to my room, but I went to his room to check instead. I opened his door and there wasn't a thing out of place. The bed wasn't made perfectly, but there were no clothes on the floor and not a dish in sight. Then I opened the closet. Dishes, shoes, and clothes—clean and dirty—came tumbling out. I slammed the closet door and barreled down the stairs.

I strode into the family room with a red face and a racing heart and yelled at the top of my voice, "Dad, if you don't make Mark get up there right now and clean up everything he just threw in his closet, I'm leaving!"

Dad slammed his hand down on the arm of the couch and screamed, "Mark, get upstairs right now and clean up your mess." Then, he turned to me. "Letha, never threaten me like that again!"

Talk about dysfunctional. I had taken on the role of mother and threatened my dad like a wife. Dad reacted to my unhealthy comment out of his own pain, and we were all a mess. I left the room crying, Mark stormed upstairs, and Dad—who knows what Dad did. It was ugly.

Suzy said, "Letha, I'm sorry that happened to you. You're that teenage girl, you know. You were living pushed out of good time and took on responsibilities you were never intended to have. Your dad struggled to parent you kids after your mom left, and it was natural that there was a triangulation between you, your brother, and your dad. I'm so glad you remembered that story and shared it with me. What do you make of that story now?"

"I can see that my powerlessness after my mom left pushed me into roles that helped me cope, and, honestly, created some good feelings for me. I learned to control things around me, rescue people who needed me, and I think I even created drama just to feel some kind of emotion."

Suzy sat back in her chair. "I think you're right. I'm so proud of you for continuing to retell hard stories from your childhood that hold intense feelings for you. You're getting to the roots of your shame and powerlessness by doing that."

Although I was healing the past, both with counseling to deal with my childhood pain and with my redeeming ladies to create fresh experiences, I continued to educate myself on the depth of just how insidious my codependency really was. The book Suzy gave me helped a lot.

I had heard it said that hindsight is 20/20. It was true. When my relationship ended with my drug of choice—a person, I got clear in my thinking. I began to see how unhealthy I had been and how crucial it was for me to heal my past wounds so my pattern of codependency wouldn't repeat itself. I was sure to repeat it if I didn't repair it.

I was learning that, as a people pleaser, I often lost myself in relationships. I didn't feel whole without a friend. When my friendship with Ruth ended, I felt especially lonely, and I couldn't believe I was going to do life without her. It was as if I'd lost a part of myself (one clue the relationship was not healthy).

I recognized I had been caretaking all the way back to my little brother. I based my self-esteem on caring for others. I was a great fixer. Caretaking gave me a sense of purpose and worthiness. Being needed made me feel worthwhile.

I was coming to understand through counseling that I had a significantly unhealthy need for validation. I relied on others, and especially my friend, to tell me that I had value. As a result, I stayed in that unhealthy relationship to feel valuable and worthwhile. I relied on Ruth to quiet my deep-seated fears of being unwanted, which made it very hard for me to accept the end of the relationship. Without external validation I felt defective and insignificant—the very feelings I felt when I was thirteen and my mom left me.

With Suzy's help, I continued to process my teen years and realized that, even then, I always needed to have someone to feel complete. I swung from one relationship (usually long-term and needs-satisfying) to another. I didn't have many days as a teen without a boyfriend to validate me.

The work I was doing, healing my past and sharing experiences with new healthy friends, was all part of what needed to happen to break down the familiar patterns of codependency in my life caused by unmet needs and lack of bonding in my childhood.

I was finding that letting go and moving on after my friendship with Ruth ended was a painful and lengthy process, especially because of my codependent traits. People-pleasing, caretaking, and my need for external validation made it challenging for me to release my dependency on Ruth. Helping her always gave me those "feel good" feelings I had when I was a kid and "saved" my little brother. I was discovering, as I healed, that I could create boundaries and set limits for myself and still use my gifts and talents to come alongside people and support them. I was gradually gaining a stronger sense of who I was as an individual because of the time and energy I was investing in getting to know myself. Honesty was healing me. Honesty with myself, that is.

"Letha," Suzy said as she stood and walked me to the door that Tuesday afternoon, "you're becoming the super-hero in your own story."

I felt fatigued after a vulnerable hour. "I want that. I hope you're right."

Icing on the Cake

C hange requires a decision, a plan, and then lots of action. The effort I made to create the original redeeming plan and invite others into the process was crucial for me, but the accountability I had set in motion, without even realizing it, made all the difference as the months unfolded. I might not have continued with the plan without my friends' involvement, as I was hurting and not always motivated to be social.

Honestly, I would see a redeeming day coming up on the calendar and dread the thought of it. I was more comfortable isolating than spending time with people. Seclusion was a vicious cycle. I would keep to myself because I feared being hurt, but I would feel more afraid when I was alone. Redeeming days were part of my slow healing process whether I felt like participating in them or not. So, I kept at it.

This spring morning, I drove across town to spend a redeeming day with Kristi. The buds were starting to break open on some of the trees as Washington's cold winter yielded to the sun's warmth. The soft white blossoms were a reminder that what seemed barren comes back to brilliant life. I smiled when I pulled into Kristi's driveway and glanced up at a beautiful Japanese snowbell tree covered with big white blooms.

I didn't know Kristi well when I asked her to help me redeem my adolescence. I had observed her from outside her inner circle and recognized that she was someone I wanted to know better. I watched her invest time and energy into her home and family to create warmth and love. I knew a little bit about Kristi and her life story. She was a woman who had overcome adversity in her childhood too. I always felt comfortable and safe around her, which was just what I needed the year of my redemption. Only a few years my senior, Kristi was a timeless beauty, tall and slender with a honey-blond bob. She was always put together, dressing casually but classic. She didn't work outside of the home when I met her, but she treated her home with the care of a high-level executive. I respected that about her. Kristi had a plan for my redeeming day, and I rolled with it. We were going to do some cake decorating.

My pulse quickened at the memories that brought up for me. After my mom left, I stopped having cakes on my birthday. Dad would come through with a gift or two, but he didn't really have the skillset to make the birthday cake thing happen.

When it came to my healing, naming how I'd been harmed was a huge part of the battle. I was living in my present through the lens of my past. I knew the key to my redemption was connecting and engaging the two. I was able to share my painful stories, both past and present, with trusted family, friends, and my counselor, and it was changing me. It was as if my past and my present were healing at the same time. The two collided when Kristi said we were going to decorate cakes.

Some people might not care about not being celebrated with a cake on their birthday. For me, it was about remembering how it was before Mom left compared to how it was after. In our family, making a cake, putting on the candles, singing Happy Birthday, and watching the birthday girl blow out the candles was a big deal. It was her day. She was the special one. She was focused on and celebrated. That tradition went away at the age of thirteen and added to my feelings of insignificance and insecurity.

While raising Bennett, celebrations were extremely important to me. His birthday, holidays, and celebrating his accomplishments were a top priority of mine, and I just might have gone a little overboard. I wanted him to feel loved, cherished, and important—the things I didn't feel at his age. His high school graduation party was one I won't forget. I planned it for weeks, and it was a wonderful celebration. My graduation was very different.

I was eighteen, finishing up my senior year, and graduation was upon me. My high school years were good for me. I sang in the choir and competed in vocal jazz competitions, was a cheerleader my senior year with a built-in group of five fun girlfriends, and started dating Barry. We were friends before we started the official boyfriend-and-girlfriend thing. From the day we officially met, I felt like I had always known him. Barry's dad, Darrell, was my elementary school principal. I was the president of the student body in the sixth grade, so I got to hang out a bit with the principal, you know, to work on the popcorn sales. Mr. Brandenburg told me one day, "I have a son named Barry, who is president of the student body at an elementary school across town." I was eleven so that didn't impress me much, until I met Barry when we were sophomores in high school. Darrell always took credit for getting us together. I'll give him that one.

When I met Barry there was an instant connection. We worked on the school paper together, sang in the choir, and I was usually hanging around his sporting events with my cheerleading squad. He called me by my last name, Currie, and I called him Brandenburg, in a flirtatious kind of way. Story has it, I challenged him to win races at an out-of-town cross-country invitational and promised him a kiss for every first-place finish. He won five races. I will deny ever having promised that since I was actually dating another guy at the time. I did follow through with the promise, however. And that's how the whole thing got started. He told me years later that he threatened his teammates within an inch of their lives if they dared to cross the finish line ahead of him. They knew what was at stake, and they relented. Thanks, guys, I owe you.

We were both planning to attend our local community college. Barry had an athletic scholarship, and I would pay as I went. I didn't have any big college plans or a degree in mind, but going to college was what everyone was doing. First, we had to say farewell to high school.

There were 350 in our graduating class. I had gone to school with many of these friends since elementary school. I was looking forward to the festivities. Dad was coming to the graduation ceremony, and I had mailed an invitation to Mom. She had moved back to Vancouver and lived across town. I wasn't sure if she'd be there or not.

We had baccalaureate services on Sunday. Mom wasn't there. Tuesday night was our official graduation ceremony. We walked in to "Pomp and Circumstance." That song always makes me cry. Its melody and stately tempo set such an emotional tone. Something about it conjures up visions of goodbyes and hopes for bright futures. I wept as I walked down the aisle that night. I pulled myself together because Barry and I were up next to sing the national anthem in a quartet with a couple of our choir friends.

The speeches were given, the diplomas passed out, and there was nothing left to do but move our tassels to the left of our caps. The class of 1977 had graduated! Our exit song was the theme from *Rocky*. I looked out over the crowded gymnasium for my mom, and then I saw her.

She was wearing a white blazer with a black blouse. She had dyed her hair a really dark brown. It was as if she wanted to look younger, but to me, she'd aged. Mom looked so different than the last time I had seen her. I was happy but somewhat surprised she was there. I couldn't get over how I felt seeing her. It was like a stranger was at my graduation, or at least a distant relative. She was there to see me graduate, but she hadn't experienced my high school years with me at all.

She didn't see me cheer. She didn't hear me sing in the choir. She didn't know about my life or help me navigate the teenage dating scene. She hadn't seen me pin on a boutonniere or receive a corsage before a school dance or celebrated with me when I won singing competitions. She missed out on my life, and I missed out on having her in it. No wonder she felt like a stranger to me at my graduation. She was.

I worked my way through the crowd to get to her. The faint smell of cigarettes wafted through my nose as I gave her a hug. After a few minutes of chatting, I had someone take a picture of us. I thanked her for coming, gave her another hug, and she left.

Barry and I headed back to my house, made something to eat, and watched TV. There were no family celebrations, cake, or graduation gifts. My mom wasn't engaged in my life enough to make that happen.

The forgiveness work I did regarding my mom some time before my redeeming year included this story. When I made the choice to forgive Mom, I specifically remembered all the little things that seemed insignificant but weren't. Instead of saying, "Mom came to my high school graduation, and it felt awkward," I learned to engage my heart by remembering details. I remembered what she was wearing, how she looked, and even how she smelled. She wasn't the same person who had raised me from birth to thirteen years old. I didn't feel connected to her, and I definitely didn't feel known by her.

My relationship with Mom healed and changed in drastic ways after I chose to forgive her. We had a connection in my adult life that I'm convinced would have never existed were it not for the work I did to forgive her. My relationship with Mom had tenderly healed; now it was my heart and the relationship with myself I was responsible for healing.

I had spent time focusing on loving my mom; now it was the thirteen-year-old abandoned girl that needed to know she was loved. This year was about my heart.

Choosing *redeemed* as my word for the year and staying committed to the process was possibly the most life-changing thing I'd ever done besides offering up those kisses to that young cross-country runner named Barry.

This redeeming day connected the past with the present. It allowed me to think about past experiences and remember what it felt like to miss out on the importance of being celebrated, even with a simple birthday cake. Today, I was getting a cake.

I couldn't help but wonder during this redeeming day whether I could have learned cake decorating from a YouTube video. But that wasn't what this redeeming journey was all about. The time I spent with my redeeming ladies was wonderful in terms of what I learned, but the experiences were unexplainable in terms of the emotional healing I was experiencing. My redeeming days weren't about techniques in the kitchen or icing secrets, they were about connection, love, and relationship. I'm not sure what we did mattered, but spending time together did matter—in deep, healing ways.

Before Kristi and I tackled cake decorating, we had a delicious lunch and took some time to get to know each other better. The table was decorated beautifully, and I felt nurtured and cared for because of the time and effort she put into making the table and the meal so special. She said a prayer before we ate. She thanked God for this precious time together but then prayed, "Help our time spent together to feel safe. Help us learn to trust each other and know the things we share with each other will be held in confidence."

She couldn't have known how I was feeling, that I was navigating through new waters as I was learning to let go of codependent behaviors. She wouldn't have known that I was going to be slow to open up as I was rediscovering who was safe to get close to. We were just getting to know each other. Even with that prayer being said, I was cautious. I knew Kristi would need to earn my trust, and I would need to earn hers too.

As we visited over lunch, I had a thought that surprised me. *I deserve to be here.* What was that about? Was it happening? Was I allowing love in? Was I embracing and accepting the time and care reserved just for me? Was this the opposite of the feelings of unworthiness I had come into this year with? I didn't share those thoughts with Kristi that day. I kept them to myself.

Many times during the year, and most often when I was sitting in my counselor's office, I would weep at the depth of the wound that rejection and betrayal caused. How could it be that I was in my fifties, with a loving husband, a precious son and daughter-in-law, close relationships with my siblings and many friends, and still be experiencing feelings of unworthiness and shame? Honestly, it was shocking to me. That's why this journey to redeem those wounded years was so important to me. The fear of going back in time to heal my pain was not as scary as the thought of living the rest of my life holding on to these feelings of rejection.

Kristi was a great instructor. She was prepared for the lesson, having already made two six-inch cakes and her favorite buttercream frosting. She had all the supplies needed and started from the beginning by teaching me how to make a decorator bag of parchment paper. I learned about couplers, tips, and the right way to hold the decorator bag as I used each tip. We practiced making elongated shells, cornelli lace, leaves, rosebuds, and, yes, I even made roses on a stick in the air! She was patient, and I laughed, thinking of what my final creation was going to look like. Practice makes perfect, and I didn't think we had enough time for the practice I needed.

At last, it was time to move to the real cake. I glued the first layer down to the plate with frosting and then moved on to the crumb coat (the things you learn from your friends). When she taught me the secret of the warmed-up spatula I thought, *This is getting good.*

Once our cakes were frosted, we started to add the design. I was feeling almost confident at this point, having spent time practicing. We moved together, adding our shells, cornelli lace, roses, and leaves to our own cakes. I must say, mine looked okay sitting there next to Kristi's. I said, "I'm not going to have to post the 'Nailed It' photo on Facebook after all."

Kristi asked me while we were decorating, "Do you think your redeeming plan is working?" She wondered if I was feeling different after the time I'd spent so far with my redeeming ladies.

My answer was a soft, "Yes." I went on to say, "Not only have the days spent with you all been nurturing and special to me, but I've got more to go." As I answered her, I willed myself to be hopeful about how I'd feel by the end of the year.

This redeeming day was one more step forward in the journey that had begun the day I forgave my mom. Over the years, Mom moved from a condo where she lived independently to a retirement villa, an assisted-living facility, and, finally, nursing care. I was able, because of the forgiveness work I'd done, to be committed and involved in her life. I was able to love her despite her choices. I chose to go see her every week, decorate her spaces for the holidays, and attend to her needs. As she aged, my visits focused more on asking questions to keep her mind engaged, playing music to remind her of her past, and providing for her physical needs. I bought her a big bulletin board that hung by her bed and kept it loaded with the most current photos of new babies and activities of her eight children and our ever-growing family. I was the one, over the years, that put forth the effort to make her birthdays special too. I supplied cake, flowers, and presents, and did what I could to encourage as many family members as possible to show up to celebrate her. She always loved a good party. I made those choices without expectations of getting my needs met in any mother/daughter kind of way. I did those things because I was her daughter, and I chose to honor her.

I'd redeemed celebrations for my mom, I'd redeemed celebrations for my son, and now, I'd finally redeemed it for my thirteen-year-old self. Kristi and I put the final touches on our cakes, took some great photos, and boxed up mine in a pastry box she had purchased for me. Kristi didn't miss a chance to create a day for me that was sweet from start to finish. It was another day of embracing love and accepting a woman's undivided attention, and I ended up with the most beautiful cake to take home. The love was healing my wounds. I connected my past to my present and allowed memories to rise up and be felt. I was continuing to name the pain of my past stories but be transformed by the love of my present day. What would the next months bring? I had a feeling the transformation was going to be like icing on the cake.

10

Let's Do Lunch

I showed up at a quaint little coffee shop in downtown Vancouver with my iPad in my bag, grabbed a table by the window, and waited for Judy to arrive. For this month's redeeming day, Judy thought we should put on a luncheon at my home for all my redeeming ladies, and we were meeting to make plans. She came through the door a few minutes later, scanned the room to find me, and smiled big when she spotted me. We hugged tight, ordered our coffees, and sat back down.

"So, how do you go about planning a luncheon or dinner party?" I asked her, pulling my iPad out in case I needed to look up any recipes. I wasn't surprised by her answer.

"I always start with a theme!"

I had been the recipient of many themed parties at Judy's. We had met when I was sixteen through her husband,

Ed, who was my high school music teacher. Mom was gone and Judy, without even knowing it, provided love and comfort and taught me a lot about hospitality and creativity. I went to their home many times as a teenager and experienced Judy's gracious and fun personality. After Barry and I married, we continued to spend time with Ed and Judy and formed a very special friendship. I was always inspired by her imaginative flare, especially when it came to sharing a meal. I look back on those years now and realize how much of an influence she had on my life. Little did I know when I was sixteen, that forty years later I would still be learning and being nurtured by her.

Judy pulled out a folder and showed me what she'd been dreaming up for us. She had already considered recipes and a variety of fun ideas for our spring luncheon. We talked more and agreed on colors, dishes, flowers, food, and even a take-home gift for our friends. We had fun dividing the tasks and recognizing just how much we think alike. Our brainstorming session at the coffee shop was another reminder of what I missed growing up. And although my mom was absent when she should have been helping me use my creativity to plan events and create beauty in our home, other teachers presented themselves in my life. Judy was one of those teachers. Through her, other friends, and my older siblings, I had learned how to create a beautiful life inside and outside my home. What I needed to heal had a lot more to do with love and connection than it did with life skills. It was the heart of this wounded adolescent that needed healing and redemption.

A week later, Judy showed up early at my house, and the fun began. We decorated the table with yellow-and-white dishes and arranged the beautiful springtime buffet. Judy brought most of the ingredients for the menu and we put the recipes together and plated them. When everyone arrived, the room was immediately filled with warmth and conversation. Nancy, Karen, and Kristi all loved the table setting and the meal prepared for them as much as Judy and I loved creating it. We dished up our plates with the loveliest salads, passed around the basket of homemade bread, and poured the lavender iced tea.

A minute after we were all seated, I received a text message from my sister Diane.

Mom is being transported from nursing home to the hospital. Don't know what's wrong. She seems to be failing.

"Excuse me," I told the ladies, and I dialed Diane. "Hey, I'm just sitting down for lunch with some friends. Do you need me to come?"

"No, you stay for now. I can attend to Mom, and I'll keep you updated," she replied.

All but one of my siblings lived in town, so I knew they would show up and be there for Mom.

"Everything okay?" Nancy asked as I hung up.

I shared the news with my friends, took a deep breath, and worked to stay present. I was trying so hard to create "good time," but I felt like somehow Mom was threatening it again. I had to make a choice at that moment to take care of me and not abandon myself for the needs of others. It would have been so easy for me to stop what I was doing and run to Mom's rescue. My default mindset said, "Don't worry about yourself; you should take care of Mom." I felt like I was being tested. I had an uneasy feeling in my gut and had to take a couple of deep breaths to let a little tension go and relax.

Judy sensed my unease. "Letha, do you feel like you need to go? We can reschedule this for another time." All my friends nodded in agreement.

"I'm okay. I need to be here today. The other kids will be there for Mom, and I'm a text or a phone call away."

So, Nancy blessed the meal, said a prayer for my mom, and we continued with our luncheon. I struggled to stay present for the next hour, knowing my mom was at the hospital. I felt worried and anxious. I couldn't shake the thought that I needed to be with her. My mind drifted off as I remembered other times over my life that I came to her rescue when she was in a crisis.

About a year after Mom moved to Texas, the phone rang in the early hours on a Wednesday morning. I got out of bed and ran down the stairs to answer it.

"Honey," said a weak and tearful voice, "can you give the phone to Dad?"

"Mom, is that you?"

"Yes, it's me," she said timidly. "Get Dad on the phone."

I put the phone down on the kitchen table and ran into Dad's room. "Dad, Mom is on the phone. She needs to talk to you."

He got out of bed and quickly moved into the kitchen, where he grabbed the phone and said, "I'm here."

We hadn't heard from Mom in months. I couldn't figure out what was going on. I felt uncomfortable standing there listening, even though I was desperate to know what was happening. I thought, *Why is Mom calling in the middle of the night and why does she sound so . . . scared?* I walked out of the kitchen and went into the living room. It was cold and dark. I sat down on the vinyl loveseat, shaking and feeling panicked while waiting for Dad to finish his call. He hung up the phone and called out to see where I was.

"I'm in here, Dad."

He walked in looking despondent and said, "Your mom is coming home." Dad stood in the middle of the room and told me what Mom said. "She and her boyfriend had a falling out last night. He was drinking heavily, and they had a brawl. Your mom feared for her life and spent hours last night hiding in an alley behind their apartment. She was only wearing her nightgown."

I couldn't focus on the rest of the things he was telling me.

"She waited to go back inside their place until she thought he'd passed out. Your mom gathered up some things and left in a hurry. I'm buying her an airplane ticket and she'll be home tonight. I told her you kids would pick her up at the airport." He turned and started out of the room saying, "I've got to go get ready for work now. You jump up too and get the boys up for school." Then he was gone.

I sat in the dark, shivering—more because of what I'd just heard than the temperature in the room. I got up, called to wake the boys, and went upstairs to get ready for school.

Later that night, Joey, Mark, and I, along with some of my older siblings, went to the airport to pick Mom up. I sat in the back seat on the way to the airport that night, thinking my mom was coming home to us and Dad. I thought she was returning to us. I wasn't sure what Dad was thinking, and I wondered why he didn't come to the airport with us. I was hopeful that things were going to work out between them and that we were going to be a family again. I was excited and nervous about seeing her.

She walked off the plane and up the ramp toward us. I swear she'd aged ten years in the time she was gone. She looked frail, not like the mom I remembered. The first words she spoke to me were, "You cut your hair off." When she left, I had long blond hair. When she returned, I had a shoulder-length bob. I liked it. I could tell she didn't. I was glad to see her safe after hearing what she'd been through, but it didn't feel good like I hoped it would. I felt uncomfortable being with her.

We were all clumsily making our way to the baggage area when she said, "I can't wait for y'all to meet Barry." (Yes, her boyfriend's name was Barry!) None of us commented. We didn't know how to respond. She had just fled for her life to get away from an abusive relationship with her boyfriend, and she was already planning their reunion. It only took her the length of the flight home to convince herself that what she'd just been through with him wasn't that bad. It was a quiet ride home.

For the next couple of months, life was difficult. Dad was dating another woman and had no intention of cutting that relationship off for Mom. Mom needed somewhere to stay until she found a place of her own, so she moved back into our house and camped out in an upstairs bedroom. She wasn't there to reconnect with us or rekindle a relationship with my dad. She was on a mission to find a job, get a place of her own, and have Barry fly out from Texas to join her.

Those were formative times for me. I was learning all kinds of things watching my parents. I went from being raised in a Christian home with strict rules to watching my parents living in sin and making selfish decisions. My world had been turned upside down. Although I needed it desperately, I wasn't getting any counseling, and neither were my parents. We were all wounded, rejected, betrayed people looking for love in all the wrong places. We were getting our needs met however we could.

I was learning, by watching my parents, that I needed people to make me happy. I needed to be loved and be in a relationship to feel whole. I was also learning that I should look outside myself to find healing for the lonely, empty places inside of me. Those lessons became the foundation on which I built my life.

I had done some emotional healing work in my late thirties. The undoing of the lessons I'd learned growing up started as I began focusing on forgiving my mom. I began to see, both in my professional work and in my personal relationships, that unforgiveness was a greater determinant of emotional health than anything else.

With the help of a counselor, I chose one afternoon to spend time specifically forgiving my mom. My counselor handed me a legal pad and a pen. I started the process by making a list of all Mom's offenses that had harmed me. Honestly, until I sat down and wrote them out that day, I hadn't given them much thought. The list was longer than I expected it to be.

The stories were there, inside of me. I had just never allowed them to bubble up. I had lived through all those experiences, I just never gave them much thought. The second step in the process was speaking each offense out loud and saying "Mom, I forgive you for . . ." over and over and over again until the list was complete. It was a long list, and it took time. I embraced the depth of the pain that afternoon, lingered in the pain for some time, and then let it go. Through tears and a deep desire to be free of the effects of those offenses, I forgave my mom that day. I released my mom from judgment and whatever emotional debt she might owe me too. I knew I couldn't wait for my mom to ask me to forgive her. That was probably never going to happen. I decided it was time for me to be free, and I had the power to choose that freedom. The choice to forgive my mom all those years ago changed everything about how I loved, related to, and cared for her for the remainder of her life.

My mind snapped back to our luncheon when Judy asked a question. "When was there a time in your life that you all felt redeemed?" I sat and listened to my friends tell of significant and restorative times they had experienced in their lives. I was encouraged once again by my redeeming ladies and their stories of hope, change, and redemption.

That's another thing Judy taught me about great parties. She always had a plan to draw out meaningful conversation. There was love, deep connection, and even laughter as we shared stories from our past and present about the redemption we'd all experienced. As I sat at the table with the women I chose to help me redeem what my mom didn't give me, I was deeply reassured that God had truly provided them all during this season of my life to help heal the past and bring me joy in the present, even as specifically as this day.

We wrapped up a little earlier than planned, and my friends took over the job of cleaning up so I could head out and get to the hospital. I arrived to find six of my siblings sitting in the waiting room taking turns going back to see Mom. After a few days of watching Mom closely and doing more testing, the diagnosis was influenza . . . yep, she had the flu. She regained her strength in a few days and was able to return to her care facility. Funny thing, my mom kind of enjoyed hospitals. I don't think she minded those days at all. She liked the extra attention from the hospital staff, and she loved it when all her kids came around. That didn't happen as often as she would have liked. Mom wanted a close relationship with her children, but she hadn't curated or nurtured one and wasn't willing to go back and heal the past to make that happen. Her choices affected not just her but also the relationships she had with her eight children for the rest of her life.

I was learning through my counseling that I was where I was today because of the experiences I'd had and the choices I'd made. Although I had spent significant time and emotional energy forgiving my mom years earlier, I was coming to understand that forgiving Mom was completely different than grieving what I'd lost because of her. As painful as my year was, I was glad I had been forced, in a way, because of the pain of a broken friendship, to do the hard work of healing the wounded places in me. I was starting to realize the choices I was making to redeem my childhood would change the trajectory of my life.

11

Finding My Way Home

The part I loved most about *The Wizard of Oz* was when Dorothy found out she possessed the power to go home on her own. She had everything she needed in her heart and on her feet to be right where she longed to be. She felt supported by her friends who traveled with her to Oz, and she learned how to get home because of the wizard's wisdom, but she ultimately discovered *she* had the ability to find her way home. I felt a lot like Dorothy. I knew I was safe with my redeeming ladies who traveled with me, and I looked to Suzy to provide the wisdom I needed to heal. But, just like Dorothy, I had the power to find my way home and heal my childhood, right inside of me.

My trip down the yellow brick road was taking longer than I would have liked. It wasn't as simple as clicking my heels together and waking up healed. I had to actually walk with those ruby slippers, step after painful step, toward my destination. Because I was laser-focused on the pain I was feeling, days seemed like weeks and weeks felt like months. I was still able to see, however, even in the midst of my pain, that one step at a time I was moving closer to being where I longed to be. I was continuing to understand the root of my pain while in session with Suzy and during times of personal reflection. Fear was still a companion and I didn't know what was ahead of me, but I just kept taking one step at a time. As I continued to stay curious about what it took to heal my past, a recurrent theme kept popping up. Whether it was in conversations with my counselor, podcasts I listened to, or a book I read, I repeatedly heard about the concept of caring for and nurturing the inner child in me.

For the first time in my life, I was connecting to the truth that the abuse, neglect, and abandonment my younger self experienced had everything to do with how I was relating to myself and others in my adulthood. Suzy said to me in a session one day, "The beginning of your life mattered the most, Letha. Life is kind of top-heavy that way." To heal deeply, I was convinced that healing the child within me was key.

One book I read gave me a map to follow as I traveled into unknown territory—*Inner Bonding: Becoming a Loving Adult to Your Inner Child* by Margaret Paul, PhD.[5] It conveyed to me a depth of understanding about the inner child. I came to understand what was required of me for healing: a growing kindness to the little girl in the story . . . and that little girl was me.

My wounded inner child had caused me pain. The abandonment of my inner child led me to destructive beliefs and actions of codependence, shame, and powerlessness. Through inner bonding, I slowly began to re-parent myself and identify the places inside of me that were still wounded.

I recognized and began to sense the little girl inside of me and nurture her just like I would my own child. I sometimes had to look at my relationship with my son to determine how to love myself. I'd ask myself, *How would I love Bennett if he felt this way? What would I do for him, say to him, if he was afraid?* I learned to recognize and identify the feelings that would come up for me, listen to my inner child, and then respond as a loving adult. My inner-child work challenged me to get out of my head and move into my body. I had to feel the feelings instead of trying to make sense of things logically.

"Inner bonding," as Dr. Paul calls it, showed me how I could learn to nurture my inner child and offer myself the good parenting I needed and longed for. It was slow going when I first started to practice communicating with my inner child. I wasn't quite sure what it would look like or how it would feel . . . until I did it and felt it.

The first thing I had to do was feel my feelings. That was a hard thing for me. It was a lot easier to push my feelings down and numb them. I avoided situations that felt painful and realized I'd been doing that for decades. I was good at it. People, approval, busyness, and denial were some of my numbing agents. The first step to bonding with my inner child was to be willing to learn from my pain instead of numbing it, and that meant I had to feel it. I became aware of how often I avoided discomfort by numbing it in some way. I had been in protection mode for a long time, and it came naturally to me.

When I began to practice caring for my inner child, a feeling would come up for me—a funny feeling in my stomach, tightness in my chest, a feeling of fear or anxiety—and instead of numbing or avoiding that feeling (protecting), I began to have conversations with her/me. This is when I asked, either internally or out loud (if I was alone), *What's going on, Lee Lee? What are you feeling? Why do you think you're feeling that way? What do you need? What can I do for you?* I'd ask the questions I'd ask a little blond girl if I saw her sitting alone on a curb, crying. I was learning that denying those feelings when they came up for me was like walking right by the little girl and ignoring her. This realization was such an important piece of the healing process. I had experienced enough rejection to last a lifetime. I sure didn't need to continue to reject myself.

When I asked Lee Lee a question, I learned to listen for the answer. It felt kind of funny and seemed unlikely that I'd hear an answer, but I did, every time. Listening took time and patience. It also took courage. It was one thing for me to ask, *What's going on?* and another thing entirely for me to hear the answer. I shouldn't have been surprised at how often I heard, *I'm afraid.* The next step in the process was talking to God about her/me. This step was easier for me. *How can I help her, God? What does she really need? What is the best thing I can do for her?* Then I'd listen again, to God. It reminded me of when I prayed for Bennett when he was growing up. I asked for guidance, wisdom, and strength to do the right thing, but now, instead of praying about Bennett, I was praying about me. I felt small nudges and big pushes. However, doing the next right thing for my inner child wasn't about knowing what I should do, it was about making sure I followed through.

One afternoon in Suzy's office, we had a conversation about my childhood experiences and how they could be subtly guiding my adult behavior. We talked about the steps of connecting with my inner child. Suzy spent our time together helping me see that taking action on behalf of my inner child was an important key in the bonding process.

"So, Letha, you've allowed your feelings to come up, you've found out what your little Lee Lee needs, and you've asked God to show you how to care for her. Now what?"

"That's the hard part. I have a business to run, a home to take care of, and a relationship to nurture with my husband. I don't have the time to take action on behalf of my inner child."

Suzy sweetly smiled and said, "So, imagine asking Bennett as a little boy what he needed one rainy afternoon when he seemed sad, and hearing him say, 'Mom, I just want sit on the couch and read books with you' and you saying, 'Bennett, I don't have time for that, I've got more important things to do.'"

"Wow," I said through my tears. "Is it really that ugly if I don't take time to care for my inner child?"

"Letha Janelle, taking loving action toward your little rejected and fearful inner child is one of the most important things you can be doing for yourself. When you ask and listen, but don't follow through, you're abandoning yourself. Can you see that?"

As I drove home after my session, I thought about how I had been abandoning myself for a long time. I was skilled at getting my needs met outside myself by other people, but not nearly as capable of meeting my own. I needed tender, loving care to heal the wounded little girl inside of me, and I was discovering that I was the one to give her that love.

I thought back to the years I raised Bennett and the ease with which I took action on his behalf. When he was a toddler, I worked part-time. Our favorite days of the week were my stay-home days. We would sit in his room, looking out the window for as long as he wanted to sit. I'd sing to him, read books, and talk about all we spied out the window. He needed uninterrupted time with me to feel happy, loved, and secure—and I gave it. I always had a list of things to do on my days off, but nothing was more important than spending time with Bennett. I wondered as I drove home from Suzy's when the last time was that I'd given myself that kind of time. I couldn't remember.

I had a chance to put this into practice the following week. I'd spent hours working on some big projects for The Healthy Weigh, helped organize a gathering with a book club I was involved in, and accompanied Mom to a doctor appointment. I woke up on Friday of that week feeling dizzy and had a queasy stomach. I took a few minutes to do my morning journaling but needed to rush through it to meet a friend for coffee. All of a sudden, I realized—this was my opportunity to do some inner bonding. I was having inner conflict. I stopped. "Lee Lee girl, what's going on?" I waited. I heard a small voice say, *I'm weak and I'm tired and I just want to rest.*

I sat with that for a few minutes. I said, "You don't ever have to be afraid to tell me that." Calmness covered me like a warm blanket. I noticed. Then I prayed, "God, what is the loving action I should take today? How can my adult care for my inner child when I've got things to do?" I knew I had to be willing to hear the answer, and I did. I didn't actually hear Him; the answer came through me. *Stay home. Reschedule coffee with your friend and take tender, loving care of your precious self today.* This was it. I had a choice to make: Show loving action toward my inner child who was brave enough to tell me how she was feeling or reject her and push forward as I was used to doing. Disappointing a friend went against my approval-seeking personality. But wasn't that just what I was trying to heal?

I thought of Bennett and saw myself sitting at his window with him, taking all the time he wanted. I started to cry. I knew what I needed to do. "How about if we stay home today and spend some time journaling, reading, and resting? We could even get out the colored pencils and a sketchbook."

Really? That would make me so happy.

I pulled my knees up to my chest and gave myself a hug. I was taking loving action and the change in my internal emotional state was dramatic. I texted my friend to let her know that I needed to reschedule, lit a candle, turned on the fireplace, and sat down. It was going to be a great stay-home day.

Inner-child work wasn't easy as I continued to practice

it, but I knew caring for the wounds of that little girl was pivotal in my healing. Loving the child within became more and more natural as time went on. I learned to recognize a feeling, ask my inner child a question with kindness, listen for her answer, talk to God about it, and then take loving action. I kept a 3x5 card close by with the steps written out until it flowed. I was determined to have my inner-child work be as normal as other types of self-care I gave myself.

I was slowly healing because I was learning to be curious and gentle with myself. I was receiving **grace** from others and extending it to myself in ways I never had before.

I was slowly healing because I was being brutally honest with myself. **Truth** really does set you free, and I was being courageous enough to tell myself the truth and hear it from people I trusted as well.

I was healing because **time** is experience and I was choosing to revisit neglected experiences to create "good time."

Redemption was happening on more levels than I even recognized. I was allowing my redeeming ladies to help me re-experience my adolescence, and I was learning to love that little girl inside of me with a promise to never abandon her again. I was learning to mother myself and listen to my deepest needs, but most important, to respond to my needs.

There's no place like home, and I was slowly finding my way home.

12

I Love You
Just the Way You Are

I woke up earlier than normal this Wednesday morning. Karen and I were headed up the Columbia River Gorge to spend time at Bonneville Hot Springs for a spa day. I started my day differently than usual. I showered and dressed but didn't put on a stitch of makeup. Karen and I had facials scheduled for 9:00 a.m., so we agreed it would be silly to get made-up for the one-hour drive. It was a stretch for both of us to make the trip barefaced . . . I mean, what if we had a flat tire, or needed to stop for any reason? We took a chance.

I say that with a little bit of a smile on my face, but the truth is, I was facing more than just accepting my natural self without makeup that day. I was letting go of my need to please and get approval from others. I was slowly letting go of what my life looked like on the surface and was becoming more curious about what was going on inside me. My powerless experiences in my childhood had set me up to believe that I had to look like I had it all together all of the time. It's pretty clear from my history that I didn't, but I wanted/needed everyone to think I did, even God.

I was encountering more than just emotional healing this year. I was growing spiritually too. I found as I was drawing closer to myself, I was drawing closer to God. I was rediscovering—or maybe discovering for the first time— God's profound, deep, accepting love for me. I was able to see that He truly did love me just like I was, with all my flaws. No amount of makeup mattered to Him, in fact, He rather loved the bare face He created.

I pulled into the parking lot where Karen and I agreed to meet. She smiled when I got in her car and gave me a quick hug. I felt accepted and loved by her too, even in my "natural" state. I was enough just like I was. It was therapeutic to drive with Karen, looking as real as I get.

Although I came up with the plan to redeem lost time and engage four caring friends to recreate good-time experiences, I was still surprised at the level of love and connection I felt with them. If I'd had parents who were as attuned to me as my redeeming ladies were, I likely would have grown up much more securely attached. I would have learned that I was loved just like I was. That sense of being lovable—worthy of affection and attention, of being seen and heard—should have been the bedrock I built my sense of self on. Instead, because of my abandonment, I built my foundation on how things looked on the surface. It wasn't such a bad trait to know how to make things beautiful on the outside; it was just becoming more and more apparent that I had built an outward life to convince others that I was enough and worthy of love.

That theme was perpetuated in my life when, at twenty years old, I competed in a local Miss America scholarship pageant against twenty-two other young ladies and won the title of Miss Clark County. After the crowning, I was escorted backstage before the celebrations began to meet with the judges and receive some encouragement and a bit of constructive criticism to prepare me to compete at the state level. I'll never forget what one judge said: "Letha, you are and will always be Miss Clark County 1979. You have an image to uphold for the rest of your life. Whether you're at the grocery store, or, quite frankly, even going out to get the mail, you should look the part." I remember thinking, *I can do that.*

Karen and I had a lot to talk about on the drive, so much so that suddenly, I noticed we had missed our turnoff. We drove right past Bonneville without a clue. Good thing we didn't have to ask for directions to find our way back . . . we didn't have makeup on! This was my second redeeming day with Karen, and I was opening up more about the pain and rejection I was feeling because of my broken friendship. She was such a great listener, and I trusted her with my story. I was becoming more vulnerable—not oversharing and dumping on her but sharing my feelings and my experiences with her. I thought about that first book Suzy had given me, *Safe People*. Karen was a safe person.

We finally arrived, checked in, and were taken back to the locker room to put on robes and slippers to prepare for our facials, baths, and wraps. We moved from there to the relaxation room and poured ourselves a cup of hot tea. Karen was first to be called back. She stood and gave me a hug before she followed her aesthetician back. "See you in an hour or so. Have a beautiful time, Letha. I hope you really rest and relax."

It was a quiet and peaceful day at the spa. While I waited for my attendant to come get me, I drank my hot tea, closed my eyes, and took some deep cleansing breaths to try to do what Karen said, rest and relax.

"Letha?"

I opened my eyes and found my attendant standing nearby, waiting to take me back. In a quiet voice she said, "Welcome. I'm Sally. Are you ready for your mineral bath?"

I stood and followed her back to the tub area. The

room was dark except for the flicker of the candles placed around the room. Music played softly in the background and lavender fragrance caressed my senses the moment we entered. Sally said in a whisper, "Ice cold water is next to the tub along with some frozen grapes. Enjoy your soak and I'll knock quietly on the door a few minutes before your time is up."

I slipped into the tub and felt my stress start to fade away. I added a bit more hot water to the bath to get it just right. I reached over and poured myself some ice water. I leaned my head on the back of the tub and took another big cleansing breath. I knew rest was an important part of my healing process.

I was taking slow, easy breaths and I felt my muscles slack beneath the water. Alone in the room, the warmth of the water permeating my skin, I had the mental space to reflect on how I felt about appearances. When had my sense of worth become so tied to how I looked? A memory bubbled to the surface.

I was fourteen and wearing braces. I, like so many of my siblings and friends at school, had teeth that needed straightening. My brother Mark and I were wearing the tin. I'd had my braces for about a year and had another year left before they were ready to come off. I would ride my bike to my appointments, where they tightened up the wires and checked things over. I loved the trip home because the visit was over, and I felt free. I pedaled uphill to get to my appointment, but home was downhill all the way. I'd fly down the street with a smile on my face and the wind blowing back my long blond hair.

After Mom left, I had to find a way to get where I needed to go because Dad worked. We had a great bike shop in downtown Vancouver that carried all kinds of models, and I fell in love with an orange Schwinn ten-speed that was buffed to a high gloss. In 1973, Schwinn bikes were the top of the line, and this one cost $119. That was a lot more money than I had, but I was willing to work for it and make payments to own that beauty. After months of making payments with my babysitting money, it was finally mine. I felt like a million bucks the day I rode her home. I named her Annie.

The last few times I'd ridden Annie to my orthodontic check-ups, the receptionist had reminded me I had a payment due. I told her I'd let my dad know. When I reminded Dad, he mentioned something about frustration with the insurance company and their need to pay. I didn't think much of it until I'd have to remind him again the next time.

This day after I checked in, I was seated in the patient's chair to wait for the orthodontist assistant to come and check me over. When she walked in, she hesitated. The orthodontist came into the office and said to her, "Take her braces off." And then he said to me, "We've warned your dad three times about past-due payments. We are not going to be able to continue taking care of you." He walked out of the room, and his assistant started removing my braces.

I held back the tears as she quietly yanked the braces off my teeth. I felt embarrassed and ashamed. I was rejected and abandoned again. Not so much by the dentist, although I felt that too, but by my dad, who didn't care enough to make a payment, take care of me, or admit he was wrong in his assessment about what he owed versus the insurance company. His pride and lack of responsibility were now affecting me. My brother Mark was further along in his treatment and only had a few months left, so they didn't remove his.

I got out of the chair, didn't make eye contact with anyone, and walked out the door of the building. I got on Annie, started pedaling as fast as I could, and sobbed all the way home. My hair was blowing in the wind this trip too, but there was no smile on my face, and I felt anything but free. My tears at that age were much more about shame than the fact that I was going to grow up with crooked teeth. I was embarrassed and began to worry about what my friends would think and what I'd tell them. I kept a lot of things that happened in my house hidden from my friends, but I knew I couldn't hide this.

When Dad got home from work, I told him what happened. Instead of showing any kind of compassion toward me, he angrily verbalized the mistake the insurance company made and blamed them and the orthodontist for my plight. He justified his behavior and showed no remorse for his part of the story. He offered no comfort, no apology, and once again reinforced my feelings of rejection and shame. I needed my dad to stand up for me, protect me, and care about my feelings. His disconnection only added to my woundedness. He proved that day that he valued his financial condition more than the condition of my wounded heart. His actions reinforced my perception of my worth. No words were ever spoken about my braces again. Ever.

I added some more hot water to the tub and thought, *Here I am spending the day taking care of myself and I'm reminded of times no one took care of me.* It seemed like memories were surfacing more often. I wondered if it was because I understood the connection that my past played in my present and, more importantly, my future. I was trying to redeem painful and lost time from my past, but I wasn't quite sure what to even do with this one. Healing can be hard at times when you don't know what to do to redeem a painful experience. I couldn't go back and change it, and when I looked in a mirror and smiled, I was reminded of it. This is when redemption requires forgiveness, letting go, and acceptance.

Redemption for me was not about justifying my dad's behavior but understanding it with compassion. It was about acknowledging the harm his choices caused me while also considering his pain and the chaos that surrounded his life back then. I believe in my heart that if he and I could talk today, he'd say, "I'm sorry, Lee Lee. I was doing the best I could, and I failed a lot of times," and I'd respond, "I love you, Dad. I forgive you." My forgiveness of him did not make the story okay, it just released me from judgment and bitterness toward my dad.

Even on days when I was supposed to be letting go and resting from the work of healing my past, I was reminded that I could redeem time by choosing to experience it again. I knew it was crucial for me to go back to the moment of harm and sit with the heartache. I allowed myself, even in that soaker tub, to remember the feelings of that teenager in the orthodontist's chair and a daughter being neglected by her father. I had to go back to the moment of brokenness to repair it.

Even though my dad had been gone for thirty years, nothing kept me from forgiving him and becoming more compassionate toward him. My emotional work and healing didn't change the relationship I had with my dad, but it changed the one I had with myself: the most important relationship of all. Forgiveness and acceptance were perfect things to practice and remember while soaking in a hot tub. I rested with the truth that I was accepted just like I was, and I didn't need straight teeth to be loved.

About Annie—during that same year, someone stole my orange Schwinn right out of our garage. I never did find out who took her, but I forgave them too.

I heard the soft knock on the door, and it brought me back to the present. I took another big breath and pulled the stopper in the tub. I felt the water drain out and allowed myself to think about those painful memories going down the drain too. I sat until every last drop of water had left the tub. Although I had been determined to rest my mind that day, I was interested in how easily it wandered back in time. I felt like I'd opened a door that had been bolted shut for years. Walking through it now seemed natural and happened often. I knew, however, that I was still in need of more pampering and solace for my body, soul, and spirit that day. I chose to rest my mind and receive care and nurturing from my aesthetician during my facial for the next hour.

Karen and I met back in the dressing room after our treatments and put our makeup on together while we compared notes about our spa treatments. We took our time getting ready and then enjoyed lunch at the hotel.

I never had a spa day with my mom. I don't think many girls of my generation did growing up. But I also didn't get to experience getting ready for prom or a date or experiment with makeup with my mom. Those things that teenage girls do with their moms, I did by myself. When it was time to pick out a dress for prom, I went by myself. When I needed to get the right tights, gloves, and shoes for the cheer squad, I took myself. I didn't go shopping for new clothes or shoes with my mom. I didn't learn about skin care and makeup or even have her to talk to about the most personal things growing up. I was on my own. My dad would supplement financially when I really needed it, but the emotional and personal pieces of my life were left unattended.

This redeeming day was a chance for me to experience time with a loving woman doing those kinds of things. I soaked it in all day (literally) and recognized on a heart level, and even on an experiential level, that once again, I was redeeming my adolescence. I was recognizing the loss of my childhood and choosing to make it good the second time around.

As I journeyed through the year and was learning more about what it takes to redeem a broken childhood, I got better at realizing the role I played in nurturing that little girl inside of me. I was being loved and nurtured by four amazing women and going to a great counselor to process through and heal my childhood stories, but I was also discovering that I had the greatest power of all right inside of me, to love and care for me.

It's a powerful and challenging day when you come to terms with the role you play in caring for and loving yourself. Mark Nepo described it so beautifully in his *Book of Awakening*. He said, "Loving yourself is like feeding a clear bird that no one else can see."[6] I was finding out how true that was. Only I could "see" the love and attention I was paying to myself internally, but I was feeling full just like that clear bird that was eating palmfuls of seed. The challenge in feeding a clear bird is that it's all about taking complete responsibility for your own happiness. Other people can't feed your clear bird . . . only you can love yourself that way. Depending on who you are and how you were raised, loving yourself can be harder than it sounds.

During my year of redemption, I began to consciously love myself. I bought scented lotions, essential oils, the perfect candle to light while I journaled, new soft pj's, and peppermint tea. I spent time decorating my home to create beauty, bought fresh flowers just because, and started dating myself. Yep, I started taking myself on dates.

I went through a workbook, *The Artist's Way,* by Julia Cameron. She required two things from anyone who planned to work through her twelve-week course. In fact, she said in the foreword of her book that if we weren't willing to practice these two non-negotiable things, we might as well not bother with the course. They were writing three longhand pages every morning, (she called them "morning pages"), and taking yourself on an "artist date" for two hours every week. All by yourself, just you, nobody else.

Cameron explained the "artist date" a couple of ways, but what got me is when she said we were to step aside from our work to engage in simple, fun activities that would nourish the childlike spirit in us. She said although the three pages of morning writing seemed harder to accomplish, more people struggled with the artist date.

She suggested a trip to a bird shop, a children's bookstore, a flower shop, or a trip to a museum. Cameron said, "It's about thinking of our creative self as our inner child."[7] There it was again. Consider what a parent with weekend visitation might do with their children. That summed up an artist date.

The messages of healing kept coming to me. I had an inner child who needed love and I was the best one to love her. I had the ability to love, nurture, fill up, and heal the inner child in me. I was doing it and I was finding real, deep-down healing. My redeeming day with Karen was somewhat of a celebration of the kind of nurturing that was healing me. Time with a loving woman who cared, experiencing beauty in the Northwest, and a spa day that refreshed my soul.

I was starting to feel a bit more hopeful. Although I had a day of physical nurturing and was feeling refreshed, I knew I still had work to do to heal my past. There was a difference between caring for the wounded woman of the present and healing the wounded little girl of the past, but

I was committed to both. Although I took a much-needed break from the emotional work I'd been doing, I always found my pain was waiting for me when I came back to it. This redeeming day allowed me to feel better—fortified, rested, and ready to face it again. It was a rest for my weary soul.

13

Beet Stacks

We were headed to some friends' house for dinner one Saturday night, and I was going to take an appetizer. I'd found a recipe for beet stacks on Pinterest because I wanted to use the fresh beets from my garden. I printed out the recipe, purchased the ingredients, and told Barry what my culinary plans were.

Barry loves the kitchen, and he loves preparing food for people. As a trial attorney he deals with conflict every day, so creating meals and serving others is his happy place. Because of his passion, I've sat back and acquiesced more times than not, to allow him his escape in the kitchen. This wasn't one of those times. I was excited about my beet stacks with goat cheese and proud that I was using my own fresh beets. I even went and bought the perfect rectangle platter to line them up with the skill of a chef on *Chopped*. I was ready, and it was my turn to create something wonderful in the kitchen.

I'd harvested the beets from the garden earlier in the week and set aside time Saturday morning to roast them. After I pulled them out of the oven and let them cool, I gathered up all the ingredients and kitchen gadgets I'd need. Barry hadn't paid much attention to what I was doing up to that point, but suddenly, he walked into the kitchen and said, "Okay, is this all I need to make the beet things?"

I did what I was used to doing—I acquiesced. Instead of using my voice and standing up for myself, I shrunk back, stepped away, and started sweating. With a flat tone, I mentioned what I was planning to do with a small round cookie cutter and how the beet stacks were supposed to look. He said, "Oh, I was thinking I'd make them look a little more earthy." I kept the peace and got smaller.

One of the things I didn't experience in my teen years was watching my parents communicate with each other. I didn't learn strategies to resolve conflict and wasn't taught how to stand up for myself. I never felt safe enough to have difficult conversations with my dad, so, instead of speaking up and sharing my opinion as anyone should, I kept quiet. I kept the peace in our house and felt it was my job to create harmony. My dad couldn't handle a rebellious teenager, and my brothers needed stability. I took on the role of peacekeeper and didn't mature in areas of conflict resolution or communicating what I wanted or needed. Here I was in my fifties, struggling with the same issues. I was still insecure about expressing my feelings or sharing my thoughts in my personal relationships.

When you combine my immaturity in communicating my opinion with being married to a husband with a strong personality (type one on the Enneagram), you've got the perfect conditions for staying stuck in that immaturity. Add to that scenario being the seventh child of eight and things get more complicated. Heck, I was forty-two years old before I realized I didn't like pickles on a hamburger. When you're raised in a herd, you catch the burger being thrown to the back of the station wagon going through the drive-through with your family. You thank God your brothers didn't intercept it on the way back and then eat it with a grateful heart. Pickles or no pickles, I didn't have a say. You eat what is put on the table and you don't ask for what you want. You learn to take what you get without speaking.

When Barry and I started dating, he provided a safe place for me with his strong and steady personality. I didn't recognize it in myself then, but I was always looking for strong and steady. I grew up experiencing extreme emotional highs and lows, depending on how my parents were doing, then I was thrown into more chaos when Mom left and Dad started dating. Barry was a rock with an even temperament and consistent personality, which was just what I needed.

We married when I was twenty-one. I'd been practicing homemaking since I was thirteen, so I didn't have trouble in those first years adjusting to being married or caring for our home. We started our life together and, even though I had a helpmate now, I was still self-sufficient and independent. You've heard it said, "You teach people how to treat you." Well, I would have been considered "low maintenance" by the way I behaved. I "taught" Barry that I was capable and tough because on the outside, I was. I didn't understand until many years later that I was fragile and broken on the inside.

I perpetuated my self-sufficiency, even when it wasn't what I really wanted. I was always the one who, when asked, "Do you need some help with that?" answered, "No, I've got it." I didn't make a big deal out of my birthday, although I secretly wished someone else would. I never asked for what I needed emotionally, because, quite frankly, I didn't even know what I needed. I'd been taking care of myself for so long, I didn't know how to let someone else care for me, even though I was desperate for that kind of attention.

The fear of being disappointed and rejected by the people closest to me ruled my behavior. I was desperate for love and attention, but afraid of it at the same time.

I still struggled with asking for what I wanted. I'd been married for over thirty years, and I was still playing the role of peacekeeper.

Barry started slicing the beets, and I turned and walked out of the kitchen. I went outside to the garden, turned on the hose. . . and started weeping. I had done so much work with my inner child to heal the wounds that held me back, but I realized at that very moment I was abandoning myself again. I should have said, "Hey, hon, I really want to make these. I'd like to prepare the entire appetizer if you wouldn't mind," but I didn't. If I had, Barry would have said, "Oh, okay, go for it." But instead, I said nothing, he heard nothing, and I felt sad, abandoned, controlled, and insignificant. My inner child shouted, "I want to be heard, I don't want to be controlled, and I want to do this myself!" But I did nothing. I allowed my wounded child to shrink back instead of having my healthy adult do the talking. I abandoned myself.

Walking back into the house, I felt defeated and manipulated. Isn't it sad that I would use those words when Barry did nothing? He just did what he does. Well, he didn't read my mind, I'll give you that, but he was innocent in the story. He was being strong and consistent.

Then I saw the beet stacks. Sitting on the perfect new rectangle platter were five piles of, let's see, what did he call them, "earthy" stacks of something. That's when I lost it!

They were the ugliest beet stacks I'd ever seen, and I was so disappointed in myself. I felt like such a wimp, and I didn't want to be a wimp anymore. I hit the granite counter with my fist and barked, "I wanted to make the beet stacks. I grew the beets, found the recipe, printed it off, and even bought the perfect rectangle platter to put them on! Why did you have to take over? Can't you ever let me do what I want to do?"

His eyes got big, he took a step back and said, "Wow, honey, why didn't you tell me that? Why didn't you use your voice? When are you going to start using your voice? I thought you said you're learning to use your voice?" (Okay . . . I got the message.)

I squeaked through my tears, "I want to redo those." Speaking up for myself felt awkward and uncomfortable, even with Barry.

He turned to leave the kitchen. "Go for it!" His tone wasn't sweet, it was full of disappointment and frustration. Of course it was. What was he supposed to do with all of that anyway?

He went into the living room. I sniffled and sighed and took his "earthy beet stacks" off the rectangle plate and disassembled them. I washed and dried the plate and set it aside. I got out my cookie cutter and cut the beets-and-goat-cheese mixture into perfect one-inch rounds. Then I stacked them, about six layers high. They were works of art. I lined them with precision on the white rectangular plate and put a tiny sprig of rosemary on top of each stack. They were truly Pinterest-worthy. I carried the plate into where Barry was sitting and sheepishly showed him my creation. He said, "We could have posted a before-and-after with 'Nailed it!' under the photo of my beet stacks."

That was nice of him to say, and he meant it, but oh, my lack of maturity, my lack of being loving and kind to myself put a big damper on the Pinterest-worthy beet stacks. We went to our friends that night and took my pretty appetizer. They said, "They're too pretty to eat." I thought, *They are now . . . you should have seen them an hour ago!*

Relationships are complicated, but truth isn't. I was learning how to love, nurture, and care for myself, and my actions and responses were beginning to come out of a good and healthy place. When I didn't pay attention to my healing, they'd come out of an immature and wounded place. Although my mom had abandoned me, I had a bigger responsibility now, to not abandon myself. That girl who stalled in her maturity at thirteen was finding her voice. It didn't sound as strong and convincing as I wanted it to, but I was getting there. It wasn't so much about finding my voice as it was about giving myself permission to use it.

As I moved through the year and attended to the wounded teen in me, I was becoming more at ease with attempting those very things I'd missed out on. I was practicing my ability to resolve conflict with others, and, all the while, I was discovering a little bit more of me. I was gradually developing more courage to speak, express, and let myself be heard, and I was doing a better job sharing the kitchen with Barry.

14

It Takes Years to Master the Art

T he year was half over, and I was feeling a little
panicked. I'd given myself a false deadline to redeem
my adolescence. My plan? Focus on my word redeemed
for the year and in twelve months (twelve easy steps) I'd be
redeemed! Things weren't going as planned.

I wanted order and certainty with my redemption.
I wanted to start at the bottom of the ladder and climb
straight to the top. I wanted to read a book about healing
the inner child and have the inner child healed. I wanted
to listen to the podcast about forgiveness and embrace it
immediately. I found that healing wasn't like that at all. I
had to allow myself to accept where I was, not pushing

myself to feel a certain way or heal faster than I could. I was learning to trust and accept the process. That was easier said than done for me.

Nancy lived about forty minutes away from my house, so I had time to think during my drive there. I reflected on the redeeming days I'd already experienced and how each one built on the other. Not in a curriculum kind of way, but in a healing kind of way. I wasn't taking the lessons I'd learned about making roux and frosting cakes and integrating those skills into my life, I was responding to the love I'd received from my friends and allowing my heart to heal. Just like a dim light brightening, I could see myself trusting a bit more and being a bit more courageous with my healing process. I was naming the stories of my past and healing them while I allowed love in. I was aware as I drove to Nancy's that I was feeling less anxious and more eager about this redeeming day than I had in the past months.

When I arrived, she took me on a tour of her beautiful home. The gallery of family photos on the wall, the antique hutch full of hand-painted china, and the attention to detail throughout her home reflected Nancy and her life. I moved slowly as she pointed out special items that all seemed to have a story surrounding them. She poured us glasses of iced tea and we took our tour outdoors. Nancy had a vegetable garden to write home about. I loved seeing what she planted and secretly coveted the drip system that kept her garden boxes watered all summer. It was a beautiful day, so we lingered outside, sitting on a bench next to the garden. I was learning to anticipate these unhurried times with my redeeming ladies. Even though I had originally asked them to spend a morning or afternoon with me, they each reserved the entire day when they knew they were spending time with me.

Nancy, having painted china and instructed others for years, thought it would be fun to teach me about how it all worked. I was relieved when she said it took her years to master the art. This lesson was just about fun.

She showed me her paints, the oils, and the brushes. With her delicate instruction, I painted and worked on lettering. I learned quickly that when you paint china, you can practice, make a mistake, and then wipe it away. I did a bunch of that. There were no expectations about my china-painting proficiency from Nancy, and that was a good thing. I was having a new experience with a friend, practicing, making mistakes, erasing them, and beginning again.

"That's what I loved about teaching china painting," Nancy said with a smile. "No matter how many times my students made a mistake, they could just wipe it clean and start again."

I stopped painting and looked up at Nancy. "I feel like I am doing that with my healing too, Nanc. I want to do it right or do it in the right order. That makes more sense to me with my structured personality than taking one step forward and falling back two. I don't like that I feel really good one day and the next day I'm triggered by something that causes me to feel rejected and anxious all over again."

"Well, maybe this day is supposed to teach you more than just how to paint china, do you think?"

I smiled and nodded. Breakthrough, recovery, redemption . . . there were so many words that were describing my year. Although healing was happening, it was like a slow dimmer switch. I wasn't even aware at times that the light was coming on. I was having small breakthroughs, I was recovering one day at a time, and I was redeeming my childhood with each intentional decision. Between the deep and personal healing with my counselor and the significant redeeming days with my friends, a dim light was breaking through the darkness.

I knew the lessons I was learning about myself and my wounded past could not have happened any quicker, but I wanted to paint the china plate and have it look beautiful now. I didn't want to make a mistake, wipe it clean, and start again.

Nancy thought it would be meaningful to work on a piece of china with the Bible verse I'd chosen for my year of redemption—Isaiah 43:1. "But now, this is what the LORD says—He who created you, Jacob, He who formed you, Israel: Do not fear, for I have redeemed you; I have summoned you by name; you are mine." We personalized it on my piece of china to say: "Letha, I have redeemed you, I have called you by name; you are mine." She painted the flowers; I painted the letters.

We sat down to a wonderful Thai-inspired luncheon Nancy had prepared for the two of us. We had Thai chicken soup, rice-paper salad rolls, and fresh fruit for dessert. She saved some ingredients so that I could make a couple of salad rolls to take home for my Friday night date with Barry. They were full of fresh ingredients from Nancy's garden, right down to the edible pansies.

Our conversation over lunch was all about our kids. We talked about the contrast between Nancy parenting four children and me only one. I told Nancy that I was learning a lot about my parenting style as I was healing and re-parenting myself.

She sat back in her chair, took a sip of tea, and said, "Tell me more."

"Well, my rearing of Bennett in his teen years couldn't have looked more different than mine. My dad was dating, my mom was living across town with her boyfriend, and I was starting high school. There was a drastic difference between the scenario I lived as a fifteen-year-old and the life Bennett lived at fifteen. I look back now and understand why I swung as far as a mom can swing to make sure he didn't experience the abandonment and lack of, well everything, that I experienced from my mom."

"Of course you did, Letha."

"Nancy, honestly, I think it's a moral and responsible thing for me to deal with my stuff. I believe the most responsible parents, spouses, siblings, and friends are the ones who do what they must do to heal their own pain. I'm determined to be one of those responsible parents, even though my opportunity to parent Bennett as a child has passed me by. I don't get to go back and wipe away those mistakes."

Where I missed out on my adolescence, Bennett, because of my over-parenting, could have prolonged his. Where I felt unsafe because I was abandoned, I communicated to him in subtle or not-so-subtle ways that he wouldn't be safe without me looking out for him. Parenting Bennett from a place of my own abandonment meant that I needed him to need me. I got my needs met by being the mom to him that I needed. I did all that subconsciously, of course. I was innocently doing what made sense. My parenting style was birthed out of my childhood story.

Bennett and I laughed uncomfortably about it when I apologized for the helicopter blades that hovered over his head his whole life (I'm still working on detachment). During one of our vulnerable conversations, Bennett said, "Mom, I'm the by-product of your abandonment."

He's right—he is. Instead of me being secure and free to hold the parenting reins loose, I fashioned security by hovering over his life. I'm not saying if I had it to do over again, I'd be less involved. I guess I'd just recognize my unhealthiness in the relationship and heal it to stop the harm that my story caused my son.

Not only did I create a model as far from the way I was parented as I could, but in some ways, my parenting style was a generational thing. The kids in my generation did more to take care of themselves because of the way our parents raised us. We woke up in the summer at 5:00 a.m. and picked berries to earn money for our school clothes. We bought the first old cars we would drive. We certainly weren't going to make our kids work that hard. We made sure to give them all the things we didn't get. Now, we question the decisions of the millennials, and we are the ones who shaped them. Won't it be interesting to see how they raise their kids?

I look at my son and the life he lives, serving God, loving his wife fiercely, and doing justice as an attorney, and I can't say that my woundedness messed him up too much. I do believe that he continues to search for his true identity and his worth because of the image he tried to live up to as my son. I know he has struggled with the expectations of his parents, even as an adult.

Although I was learning that mistakes could be made with china painting and erased, my parenting of Bennett was permanent. I left an imprint on his life that can't be wiped away. Redeeming time was teaching me, however, that it's not too late for either one of us to heal and grow into more of who we were created to be.

I'm thankful that Bennett and I can have honest conversations and that he continues to extend grace to me while he pursues his own healing, emotionally and spiritually. I'm flying a lot higher these days since Bennett got married. I can't say it was easy for this helicopter pilot, and I'm sure I owe my sweet daughter-in-law a few apologies, too, but thankfully, we are all seeking God's best for our lives and our families.

Nancy and I finished our lunch and put the finishing touches on my china piece. It was beautiful. She was going to fire it in her kiln and give it to me the next time we saw each other. Nancy gathered up my take-home box with spring rolls, walked me to the door, and gave me a big hug. "You're doing a great job, Letha. I'm proud of you. Remember, don't be afraid if you make a mistake; just wipe it clean and try again. You'll end up with a beautiful piece of art."

I drove home thinking, *Who I spend my time with and how I spend it are some of the most important decisions I am making on this healing journey.* Nancy, having spent years in the Word and traveling through life's ups and downs, was just who I needed to be investing my time with. Her wisdom, birthed out of her experiences, was an encouragement to me. I realized I was learning to trust more. Trust was a process for me. Although I asked these friends to share in my year of redemption, I wasn't ready early on, because of my own pain and lack of trust, to open up and share my story with them. Slowly, as the months passed, I was setting up new boundaries for myself about what was important to share and what was mine to process alone. As I healed, I shared different things with God, my counselor, and Barry. I shared and engaged the parts of my story that were important for me to tell another person with Nancy that day. Redeeming my adolescence had so many layers. Trusting people close to me and not fearing rejection or abandonment were big ones.

Somehow, deep down in my wounded soul, I had a belief that if I shared things about myself that didn't look attractive or weren't good, I'd be rejected again. That was a lie I had lived with and functioned out of for most of my life. I was learning to trust . . . possibly for the first time in my life. I trusted the people that were showing themselves to be reliable and safe. I was learning to trust myself too.

As with every redeeming day spent with my friends, I left Nancy's house feeling less anxious. I felt more hopeful and okay with making mistakes, wiping them clean, and starting again. I was also accepting that I couldn't erase mistakes I'd made in my past, but I could redeem and heal the consequences of those mistakes and create a better future.

141

15

Just Bee—cause

"What are you doing today?" Barry swiveled his chair to face me and took another sip of his morning coffee.

"I have a redeeming day with Kristi."

"Oh good, are you bringing home another cake?"

"No." I chuckled. "I'm not sure what she has planned for me today. I never know until I show up."

We were sitting in our bedroom where we'd sat every weekday morning for years, having our first cup of coffee and enjoying the view. Barry's whimsical handcrafted birdhouses were just outside the window nestled under the vine maple. He kept them full of food for the birds, but mostly for the squirrels. We loved welcoming the day by watching the different species of birds. A small hummingbird feeder was attached to the window closest to Barry's chair, and we had even named the little birds that frequented that feeder.

He glanced back out the window. "You don't know the plan, huh? That's different for you." Then smiling and looking back at me he said, "You're usually the one in charge."

"I know. It feels uncomfortable every time I go, but it's getting easier."

"Hon, I'm impressed that you're following through with this redeeming day thing. I think it's making a difference."

"Why do you say that?"

"You seem happier. I feel like between what you've told me about your discoveries in your sessions with Suzy and the days you're spending with your redeeming friends, you're getting better."

I felt a big lump in my throat. "I wish I could say that I wasn't in pain and didn't feel rejected anymore, but I still do. This is just so hard." I fought back a tear and spoke with a quieter voice. "It's like a one-day-at-a-time thing for me. Even though I know that breaking off my friendship with Ruth and addressing my codependency has a lot less to do with my todays and much more to do with my yesterdays, today is the day it hurts."

"I'm sorry you're hurting, honey. But remember, the biggest rewards usually come from having the courage and perseverance to create your own path, and that's what you're doing." He stood up and said, "Give me a hug."

I stood and hugged him. My head rested just below his chin, and I lingered there until he whispered in my ear, "I've got to get in the shower now, but I'll look forward to hearing about your redeeming day tonight at dinner."

I pulled into Kristi's driveway around 11:00 and looked up to see two hanging flower baskets flanking both sides of the double garage doors. They were full of purple and white petunias, and the flowers hung so low they almost touched the ground. Kristi opened the door before I even got out of the car. She greeted me with the biggest smile and had a little squeal in her voice. "I'm so glad you're here."

I gave her a hug and said, "Thanks for doing this for me."

"Oh, Letha, I'm so honored to be a part of your redemption story. Come in, I'll show you what I have planned for us today."

"Not just yet. Before we go in, I've got to know, what's up with your hanging baskets? They're glorious."

"Miracle Grow, every Sunday, never fail," Kristi said with a satisfied smile. "My goal every year is to get them to touch the ground."

As I followed Kristi inside, I chuckled. "Well, I think you're going to reach your goal this year."

145

The table was set for lunch. I stood and took it all in. There were little black-and-yellow bumble bees peeking out of the fresh flowers in the middle of the table. Bumble bees were on the stir sticks resting in the tall iced-tea glasses, and atop the jar filled with raw honey too. There was even a handcrafted gift box next to my place adorned with yellow-and-black bees. The dishes were creamy yellow and white with a touch of black . . . it was perfect. Kristi announced, "The theme? Just Bee-cause. You're loved just because, Letha. Just because you're you."

Just because—that was how I needed to be loved. Not because of what I did or how good I was at something—just because. It was a thoughtful and perfect theme for a little girl looking to redeem a love she'd lost. It was a perfect theme for a little girl who grew up needing to perform for recognition and believed she couldn't hold on to a mom's love no matter how good she was.

I shook my head. "Kristi, this is just what I needed today."

"I'm so glad. I've enjoyed every moment preparing for you. Are you ready for lunch? I made one of my favorite dishes, stuffed summer squash. It's just come out of the oven."

"I wondered what smelled so good. I can't wait to try it."

We sat down to lunch and had a fun conversation. We shared the same love for interior decorating and creating beauty in our homes. Afterward, we took a walk through her exquisite backyard. I noticed the changes in scenery since I was there earlier in the year. Kristi and her husband saw landscaping as a labor of love. The flower beds were freshly bark-dusted and free of weeds, and the grass was as lush as a golf course.

"Kristi, how do you and John keep your grass so green? And there's not a dandelion in sight!"

"Oh, that's been a process. We learned that destroying developing flowers before they mature prevents them from germinating. We apply weed killer in the fall and it moves directly to the roots, which gets rid of the darn things permanently."

Of course, I thought. "Gardens can teach us a lot," I responded. "I'm learning about getting to the root of my problems too."

We finished our stroll through the yard and headed back into the house. Kristi was excited to show me what she had planned.

I followed her into the dining room where she had a craft project prepped. Kristi was a Stampin' Up demonstrator and thought it would be fun to create a piece of art with my word for the year. She had chosen scraps of colored paper that beautifully accented my rustic lodge home. There were die cuts and stamp pads, embossers, and colored pencils. I was about to have an art lesson. Before we got started, she had one more surprise.

Sitting at my place at the table was a black leather book with REDEEMED embossed on the front. She said, "Open it, and take your time." She left the room and gave me some time alone.

I'm not sure how long it took her to put it together, but it was magnificent. It was a scrapbook revisiting each month I'd spent so far with my redeeming ladies. The letters I'd written, the pictures I'd taken each month, and much more were on each delicate page. I grabbed a Kleenex out of my purse and dabbed my eyes. I was reminded as I turned each page, of the sacrifices my redeeming ladies had made for me. I realized, by looking back to the beginning of the year, just how far I'd come. It was a powerful thing to see all those experiences represented in one place. My redeeming days seemed diluted because they were spread out over the year, but viewing them together like this, they felt potent. I read each letter I had written and noticed the change in my tone as I flipped through the pages. Proof of my healing was right there in those letters. I thought back to what Barry had said earlier that morning about how he was seeing changes in me. I was seeing them now too. I don't think Kristi could possibly have known the significance of her gift.

She stepped back into the room and asked if I'd had the time I needed with my scrapbook. "If you'll leave it here with me, I'll keep working on it as the year unfolds," she offered. "In the end, you'll have a way to remember this year."

"Thank you, Kristi. It's a priceless work of art. I'll treasure this. And this was important for me to see today. Sometimes it's hard for me to recognize how far I've come in my healing." I picked up the book and said, "I can see it here."

"I didn't even think of that when I was creating it for you. I'm so glad you like it."

It was time to get started on our art project, and Kristi was the ultimate teacher. She showed me how, watched me do it, and checked in with me to see if I felt good about it. Each letter in my word of the year came to life on a three-inch square that I carefully stamped, embossed, and antiqued. I used sponges and pokers and all kinds of stamps. I glued and dotted and created until I had my word complete. When I was all finished, Kristi asked if I would leave it with her so she could have it professionally matted and framed. My redeeming ladies didn't do anything halfway. They took the job of helping me redeem my adolescence very seriously, and I was the beneficiary of their love.

Kristi and I had time to talk and share about the growth both of us were experiencing. We were each so thankful for that year. Kristi told me that our time together to help me heal and grow had been equally important to her. John Gottman, author and research psychologist said, "Trust is built in the smallest of moments."[8] And that was happening with Kristi and me. From the very first redeeming day we spent together, she had shown me that I could trust her. She

149

was reliable, and more importantly, I knew she'd hold my words and thoughts shared in confidence. Her generosity with her time and her financial investment showed me that she believed in my quest to redeem time. I deeply valued her part in my story.

I finished up my craft project and realized that I had meditated on the word *redeemed* for hours. It somehow felt like more redemption happened even as I struggled through the art project that came so naturally for Kristi but was a learning process for me. What we focus on, we become.

On my way home, I thought about my one-day-at-a-time journey. This day was a good one. It was a day of love and connection. It was a day of remembering how far I'd come. It was a day of cultivating healthy friendships, and I hoped it was another day closer to my redemption, just because.

16

Sister Day

I had an unexpected redeeming day with my four sisters. The five of us made it a priority to spend time together as often as possible. My sister Nancy lived in southern Oregon and was coming to town, so we planned a day at my house to hang out. They didn't realize it, but I had an agenda. . . to make amends.

For the last fifteen years, whenever we had a sister day, Ruth had been invited too. She became part of the family from the very beginning of our friendship and attended all our events. From the more intimate times with my sisters to the larger gatherings with extended family, Ruth was welcome. I always included her in our parties and celebrations.

As I continued my counseling and understood more about my dependence on Ruth, I saw why I had needed her to be a part of all the areas of my life. I relied on her help, and I needed her reassurance and support to feel secure. That feeling grew over the years and became a way of being for me. As I healed, I realized I had missed out on building relationships with my sisters in the last fifteen years because of that.

I had many conversations with Suzy about my sisters. I was deeply devoted to them but was never dependent on them, even as a teenager. They were all actively participating in their own lives with spouses, children, and grandchildren. I had healthy relationships with my sisters but regretted the opportunities I'd missed because of the amount of time I had spent with Ruth. I felt like I needed to redeem that time too.

My two oldest sisters Linda and Diane rode together and arrived first. Bailey and I greeted them at the door, and I warned them to take notice that she was right under their feet as they stepped across the threshold. "Good morning. I'm so happy you're here. Come in, I'll take your coats, and the coffee has just finished brewing."

Linda smiled as she hugged me and handed me her coat. "I saved my second cup. I knew you'd have a fresh pot ready for us."

"I expected to see Ruth's car out front. Is she coming?" Diane asked with some curiosity.

"No, she won't be here today. I have more to tell you about that later."

I was five and six years old when my two oldest sisters got married. Our relationships changed over the years as I went from being a child to a woman. I was their number one babysitter as their children grew up, and I always felt like I was a part of their families. Later in my life, they both offered support and mentoring in my professional world. I was there for them, and they were there for me. I hadn't shared as much about my redeeming year with them as I had with Nancy and Vickie. I knew they would be surprised by what I had to say.

The front door opened, and the next two sisters came in with big smiles. "Sister," Nancy said, hugging me. "It's so good to see you. Can you believe we're all together? How long has it been?"

"Too long," I said softly in her ear as I hugged her back.

Vickie said in her childlike voice, "Hi, girls, we're all here! This is the best!"

It is. Just the five of us. How long had it been since we'd gotten together without Ruth? Fifteen years?

We made our way over to the kitchen island, poured ourselves coffee, and grabbed one of the breakfast parfaits sitting on a wooden tray in the middle of the island. There were five bar stools, so we made ourselves comfortable while we caught up a bit and ate our breakfast.

153

We had a ritual of starting with the oldest sister and taking turns sharing about what was going on with us and our families. Before Linda had a chance to speak, I said with a weaker tone than normal, "Could I go first?"

Linda said, "Of course." Everyone was quiet and looking at me, wondering what it was I needed to share.

I immediately teared up, and although I'd thought about what I wanted to say to them, I struggled to find the words. "I've been going through a really tough time this year and I've realized that I owe you an apology." No one said a word. "Nancy and Vickie know more about what I've been going through, but Linda and Diane, I haven't shared as much with you. Late last fall, Ruth and I ended our friendship."

"Oh." Linda let out a knowing sigh.

"The circumstances don't matter as much as the pain it caused me. And because of that pain, I started digging deeper into what was really going on with me. My deep dig took me all the way back to my childhood."

I went on to explain, through my tears, what I had learned about being taken out of time as a teenager, but how time could be redeemed. I shared with them the plan I had made with my redeeming ladies to create good-time experiences and the huge awareness I'd gained in counseling since the beginning of the year.

They were silent and looked on with loving concern as I spoke. "The most important revelations in the last year have been what Mom's abandonment set in motion for me. Although I looked like I was in control on the outside and could handle things on my own, I've always had an extreme need for a mother figure. Ruth provided that for me. Letting go of our friendship has been intensely painful and extremely healthy at the same time."

Diane reached for a Kleenex. "We're listening, Letha."

"Believe me," I said with a slight chuckle, "I could take up the four hours we have left together. I don't want to do that, but I do need to ask for your forgiveness." I lifted my hand, knowing one of them, or all of them, would chime in to say, "No, you don't." I knew I had to get this out.

"I realized this morning that it's been fifteen years since the five of us were together like this. Ruth was always here. You were always so loving and welcoming with her, and I know you meant it. I realize now that I missed out. I missed out on intimate conversations that might have happened were she not there." I took a deep breath to keep from crying. "I missed out on spending time with you together and individually because I chose to spend most of my time with her. Fifteen years is a long time, and I missed out because I was too unhealthy to let go of her and stand alone. I don't believe as sisters we were meant to have an exclusive relationship, but I also know we have something really special that was affected because of my relationship with her. I'm so sorry. Will you forgive me?"

All four of them were crying as they got off the bar stools and made their way over to where I was sitting. It was a sweet group hug. Vickie was the first to speak. "I'm so proud of you. I know how hard you've been working and I'm really glad you're doing better."

I felt a sense of relief during that hug. Now I could let go of the regret and shame I felt. It was hard to be that vulnerable, even with my sisters. But because I was, they were able to be vulnerable with me. One at a time, each sister shared a little bit about how they felt about my relationship with Ruth. I didn't realize the last fifteen years had been hard on them.

I sat listening to my sisters share their true feelings with me. My honesty with them gave them permission to be honest with me. Nancy and Vickie especially were really open about how much they had "missed me" in the last fifteen years.

Vickie said tearfully, "We just wanted to be with our sister. We're so glad you're back."

"I'm not thinking about the last fifteen years," Diane said through her tears, "but the ones long before that. I think we owe you an apology. Where were we during those years when Mom was gone and you were left alone?"

Linda spoke up. "I was just thinking the same thing, Diane. Where were we?"

"You were living your lives and raising your kids. I

haven't questioned your love for me then or now through any of my processing," I said.

Nancy put a hand on my shoulder and said, "Letha, tell us more about what you've been processing in counseling and what your redeeming days are like for you."

I spent the next few minutes telling them about how my counseling sessions were helping me heal. "I've been willing to share the hard stories of my childhood with Suzy. It hasn't been easy, but it's been worth it. Between my counseling and my redeeming days, I'm healing."

Vickie said, "You're brave, Lee Lee."

I smiled. "My redeeming ladies have been amazing. The days spent with them have nurtured me and they've helped me create good-time experiences that, together with the hard work I'm doing this year, are making such a difference. It really has been a year I could write a book about."

Diane said, "I hope you do."

Linda chuckled. "Man, I'm glad I didn't go first. This has been good." We all laughed.

I said, "Who's ready for lunch?"

We moved to the dining-room table to share our meal. I volunteered to pray before we ate and there wasn't a dry eye among us. I thanked God for my sisters and the gift of this day. Truth was shared, grace was extended, and time was made good.

17

The Bat Phone

Suzy supported me through many difficulties over the year. She helped me remember important stories about my mom, guided me through current decisions about my friendships, and even edited an important letter I needed to send Ruth. She created a strong foundation for me as I grieved my losses. We had a rhythm to our sessions each week, and I became more and more comfortable as the year went on. I had a little notebook that was dedicated especially for my Suzy visits. I would take notes when I was with her so I wouldn't forget the important things she taught me, then during the week I'd write notes about things that concerned me so I wouldn't forget to share them with her in our session. There was never a time throughout the year when I felt like I was ready to stop seeing her. She was an important part of my redemption plan, and every week I realized it more.

I arrived at her office on a blustery, wet Tuesday in September. I had driven all the way in horrible road conditions and was a bit jittery when I arrived. She sensed that. Suzy started out the session by having me do some deep-breathing exercises to get me settled. It helped.

"Feeling better?" she asked when I finished.

I nodded and took one last big breath. "Yes, definitely."

She caught up on my week, then sat back in her chair. "Letha, we've spent a lot of time talking about your mom leaving and how that affected you as an adolescent. We've connected the dots from those times to your behavior now. Today, if you're willing, I'd like to talk with you about your dad for a bit."

"Sure, what can I tell you?"

"Well, when I bring up your dad, is there a story that pops into your head?"

"Oh, there's a lot." Things moved around in my stomach as if my body was taking me to a story.

I spent the next forty-five minutes helping Suzy understand more about what it was like at home after Mom left. I was so consumed with my pain and my life at the time that I really didn't have any idea what Dad was going through. He was doing what made sense to him at the time, just as I was. For months after Mom left, he would call me and my brothers from our rooms in the evenings to come sit with him, to talk and pray. It was awkward and uncomfortable. None of us, as I remember, wanted to participate, but we did it for Dad. My two brothers and I would sit in the living room, listening to Dad talk about his pain and cry through his prayers. We all cried, and then, after an appropriate amount of time, we would get up and leave him there. Even though I was engaging in something as personal as prayer and as intimate as crying, I felt disconnected from him. We didn't have a strong bond before Mom left, so we didn't have much to build on after she was gone. He needed us, so we were there for him as much as teenagers can be there for wounded parents. In many ways Dad parentified me. He needed me to meet his emotional needs, which I couldn't possibly meet, and depended on me to take over the responsibilities of the homemaker. This wasn't the same as him raising me up to contribute to household chores. It was as if I was a surrogate parent to my brothers and him.

I did my best to support him during those years even though that wasn't my job as a teenager. I took on adult behavior and did what I could to keep control of the environment around me from the time Mom left. I made lunches for Dad, kept the house clean, and sat and paid bills with him once a month too. I was shoved out of time in my relationship with Dad as much as in any other part of my life. Instead of being his daughter and being influenced by his parental love, I turned into a helpmate, a co-parent, and his housekeeper.

Things changed again for me at home when Dad stepped into the dating scene. He lost a bunch of weight and went out and bought a polyester leisure suit in every color. The baby-blue was my favorite. He bought a brand-new car, a bronze 280Z, and started wearing Old Spice cologne. There were no cell phones or call-waiting in the 1970s, so with three teenagers in the house, Dad knew if he was going to get time on the phone, he was going to need one of his own. The next thing we knew, he had AT&T come out, install a private phone line in his bedroom, and hook it up to a bright red phone. We named it the Bat Phone. (Dad didn't know we named it that.) Weird stuff started happening.

We would be hanging out in the living room on the other side of the house when we'd hear the Bat Phone ring. My dad, who we had watched lay on the couch most nights, would jump up and run through the house like an Olympic sprinter. He did whatever he needed to do to get to that phone. I think he tripped over our dog, Sugar, one night dashing to get to it before the caller hung up. He would spend hours on the phone just like a teenager. I felt like I went from living with two teenage boys to living with three. We weren't allowed to answer his phone . . . until we were.

At some point in Dad's dating scene, he hooked up with more than one lady at a time. That's when he used us to cover for him. The two women each thought they were the only one he was dating, and he needed our help to make sure that story continued. I went from my mom betraying my dad to my dad betraying the women he dated and dragging me into the story with him. Deceit and unfaithfulness were being modeled for my brothers and me. I went from a life with one set of family values to another. Things were getting more and more complicated.

The serious problems started when we would answer the Bat Phone at the wrong time or say the wrong thing to the wrong person. Dad had such a story going on with his girlfriends he couldn't keep his tale straight, much less the three of us.

He would be on a date with one and the Bat Phone would ring. My brothers and I would play rock paper scissors to determine who would have to answer the call. I hated it when I lost. I learned quickly that when you're living a life of deception, there's no right answer. It seemed no matter what I told the "left-out lady," it wasn't right. I wouldn't wait for Dad to come home to report my contribution to his story. I would just leave a note that she had called and go to bed.

All hell broke loose when our phone message didn't jibe with his story. Dad was an expert at shifting responsibility. We were the bad guys, and he was the innocent party. He blamed us for his relationship failures. The yelling, the manipulation, the deception—it was ugly. I remember one time thinking, *Wow, is this what Mom put up with? No wonder she left.*

Dad was a wounded man looking outside of himself to feel better. His new lifestyle was a distraction from his present circumstances. It was hard for him to be with his own kids when we were hurting. Spending time with us would have caused him to have to look at our pain and his. He started engaging in the lives of his girlfriends' families more than he did with us. If he showed up to watch a football game on a Friday night with his new camera, it was his girlfriend's son he'd take pictures of playing football instead of me cheerleading on the sidelines. When he didn't have time to take me driving when I was practicing for my driver's test, I'd find out at school the following week that he had taken his girlfriend's daughter driving the previous weekend. Although Mom physically abandoned me, Dad emotionally abandoned me. Emotional abandonment was about what didn't happen. Dad provided for all my physical needs—I had a warm place to live, food in the refrigerator, clothes that fit, medicine when I was sick—but he wasn't attuned to my emotional needs. His choices added to my insecurities and strengthened my belief that the people we should be able to count on aren't dependable.

I noticed while I was sharing stories about my dad that Suzy didn't take notes. She sat back in her chair, folded her hands in her lap, and just listened. When I was done and took a big deep breath, she leaned forward and said, "Letha, when you believed that the people you should depend on weren't dependable, it was a setup. You were set up to be fiercely independent. Can you see why you struggle with trusting others and at the same time look outside yourself to get your needs met?"

I nodded my head. "That's a bad combination, isn't it? I created false control around me to feel safe, but with that control, I built walls. Walls that kept people from really knowing me, and quite honestly, kept me from really knowing myself."

"This year of redeeming the adolescent girl inside of you has as much to do with your emotional abandonment from your dad as it does with your physical abandonment from your mom," Susy said. "When a parent, or in your case, both parents abandon a child, it causes internalized shame, which leads to codependency in adult relationships. I'm so proud of you for facing the pain of your past."

Suzy had a gentle smile on her face. "Letha Janelle, are you seeing that your future will be forever changed because of your courage to face your past?"

I smiled back through my tears. "I do believe that. I just wish it didn't hurt so much." I turned a page in my notebook on my lap and wrote the words "Letha, you are courageous."

18

It's Always Darkest before the Dawn

I reached over to shut the alarm off one morning, took my first step out of bed, and the room started spinning. I had vertigo. I called out to Barry to get me something to throw up in because I wasn't going to make it to the bathroom. He jumped out of bed, brought me a little garbage can and a cold rag for my head, and sat with me on the floor. The extreme dizziness didn't subside for about thirty minutes. I'd never experienced anything like that before and I was scared.

Barry felt powerless to help me. "Honey, can I get you something else? Do I need to take you to the doctor? What does it feel like?"

"Can you turn off the lights?" I tried closing my eyes, but that seemed to make it worse.

"Sure." Barry got up and flipped off the light.

Looking straight ahead, I whispered, "I'm getting a little bit better, I think. I just need to sit here until I can stand up."

I'd heard stress could trigger vertigo and it was sometimes associated with anxiety. That made me feel even worse. Vertigo feels like everything around you is spinning. It wasn't just the room around me that was spinning that morning.

It was months into my year of redemption, and the work I was doing to heal emotionally was still grueling. Although I was enjoying redeeming days with my friends, I was still spending a lot of time alone processing the pain of my childhood abandonment. I was understanding more clearly the connection between my mom leaving me and the feelings I was having about the end of my relationship with Ruth, but I wasn't sleeping well, and my body was showing signs of emotional wear.

When I was feeling a bit better and was able to stand, I showered and got dressed for the day.

Barry said, "Honey, are you sure I should leave you alone? I can stay home today and take care of you."

"I'll be fine, and I promise I won't drive a car or climb a ladder. I'll call you to come home if I need you."

So, he gave me a hug and a kiss and left for work. I

planned to lay low and do a little journaling. I didn't have the emotional or physical strength that morning to do anything else.

It might have been one of the lowest points of my "sacred journey" so far. If it was true that "it's always darkest before the dawn," then I could only hope that dawn was right around the corner. I felt more than just sad; I felt depressed. Recently, I'd been experiencing persistent loss of appetite, insomnia, and difficulty concentrating. I really didn't know if I could keep pursuing this redemption thing. Was connecting to my past pain just leading to more pain, or was it leading to healing? I wasn't sure what I believed that morning. I was so weary and still hurting so deeply that at times, I wondered if healing was even possible. My present situation of losing a friend and recovering from codependency felt in some ways worse than the pain of my childhood. I knew the unfinished business from my childhood was the cause of my unhealthy patterns in the first place, but I didn't know if I could keep fighting a fight I wasn't sure would bring about the results I was desperate for. I felt undone.

I slowly got myself settled in the back room of the house, a small office with a cozy couch. It felt like a safe space to rest that morning. Bailey jumped up next to me and snuggled in. It was as if she knew I needed her to stay close. Despite how I was feeling, I took a pen to paper and started writing. Journaling was a powerful tool to get clarity about areas of my life because it always illuminated what was going on inside of me. I needed some insight and wanted to process my scary episode with vertigo that morning. I hoped I would feel better when I was through. I knew if I didn't get some of my fear out on paper, it would just keep rolling around in my head. Remembering Suzy's encouragement to be curious, I wrote some questions in my little black-and-white composition book:

- What's motivating me to continue to heal/redeem my adolescence?
- Was my vertigo a warning sign to stop doing something?
- What will happen if I'm brutally honest with myself about my past and present pain? What will happen if I'm not?
- What will my future look like if I stop this emotional healing work and just let time pass?

I worked to answer those questions for over an hour. I found myself writing about how I'd much rather feel pleasure and happiness than pain and suffering. My relationship with Ruth, although codependent, provided me pleasure, just like so many addictions do. While I wrote, I saw why I was having such a hard time giving it up: I was trying to move away from something that brought me pleasure but wasn't good for me. I made a list of coping mechanisms other people use, just like I was using my relationship. Food, shopping, alcohol, drugs, social media—I could see clearly why *those people* should give up their addictions . . . I was just struggling to give up mine.

Oh, the clarity journaling brings. Overeating numbs pain, shopping sprees help us avoid emotional problems in our lives, and drugs and alcohol anesthetize. All addictions take root in our empty places. I saw, as I continued to journal, that I was in recovery just like anyone else fighting an addiction. No wonder it was so painful.

My journey to redeem my adolescence started because of the pain brought on by the current perceived abandonment. The rejection of a friend caused the wounded places of my childhood to fester as if those wounds were fresh. That's when my pain became a good thing. It drove me to take a closer look at the past and how it had influenced my life. For my healing to be permanent, though, I had to look at what my childhood abandonment would *continue* to cause if I didn't address it. I was sure to repeat my patterns of codependency if I didn't heal completely and redeem my adolescence.

After I wrote, I sat in complete silence for more than an hour. I was emotionally spent. No music, no sound, just my and Bailey's breath going in and out. In my stillness, I heard a voice.

171

I've heard of people hearing voices or hearing from God. I've had nudges and I've had impressions, but I can't say I'd ever heard Him as clearly as I did this particular morning. An impression came over me as if it was audible.

Letha, all the work you're doing to process your pain and heal your past, you're doing for future generations.

It took my breath away. He had me at future generations because I'd do anything for Bennett. I'd go through a lot worse pain, grieve my lost childhood, and deal with all my unhealthy relationships if I knew it mattered to my son and his family. I'd do anything for them. I knew, as depressed as I was feeling, I couldn't have conjured up that kind of whispered promise. I sat for another thirty minutes meditating on that sentence: "All the work you're doing, you're doing for future generations." Wow.

That promise was a turning point for me. It was one thing to bear this pain and do the hard work to heal the past so that I might have a healthier future, but the promise that my efforts would affect my son, his precious wife, the grandchildren hoped for, and even the generations to come after them, was what I needed to hear that morning to keep fighting the fight.

Just as my family's history and my individual story could not be separated, my history could not be separated from Bennett and his family either. He was a by-product of my abandonment, and I was determined for him to become a by-product of my healing instead.

Something Suzy shared with me in a counseling session came to mind as I was processing that day. We were talking about how far back I needed to go to heal old wounds. She said, "Letha, when something is not dealt with, especially emotional pain, it never goes away. It doesn't die; it just goes into hiding and lives on. For some people, for the rest of their lives."

I had been in denial or just ignorant about how I'd been shaped by my childhood. Philosopher George Santayana said, "Those who do not remember the past are doomed to repeat it."[9] There's truth in that . . . If I had not seen the ways I'd been shaped by my past, the odds were high that I would have unintentionally mimicked the patterns of my family of origin for the rest of my life, which would have directly influenced the generations after me.

I opened my composition book again and rewrote that first question I had answered earlier that morning: What's motivating me to continue to heal/redeem my adolescence?

This time, weeping, I wrote with confidence. "What keeps me processing and engaging the painful stories that harmed me? It's the future, that's what. To know that the work I'm doing today is going to make a difference in the lives of Bennett, Crystal, and their children. I can do this. I'm going to be okay. It's worth it."

God's promise to me that day was bigger than I realized. I thought about my clients at The Healthy Weigh—I was influencing generations there as well: moms and dads, aunts and uncles, sisters and brothers. The ripple effect of my healing was deep and wide. One choice, one painful reckoning, and one life-changing promise at a time. The dawn was breaking.

19

Heart Change

In my pursuit of healing, I was always seeking new ways to experience restoration. One day while looking on the internet, I read about a conference called Heart Change. As I looked over the description of the four-day intensive conference, I thought, *That's for me.* Their slogan was "Heart Change—Redeem Hearts, Restore Lives." I knew a sign from God when I saw one.

I went online and registered. *This is great! I'm going to have a heart change.* It's funny what you hang your hope on when you're hurting. Even though I was doing the work required to heal and knew time was part of my process, I wanted to feel better *now.* I hoped Heart Change was going to be a quick fix. I enjoyed instant gratification like the rest of society seemed to. Microwaves, instant pots, and the World

Wide Web got me what I wanted right now, and I liked it. I was learning there was nothing instant about the healing of a wounded soul, but I felt a sense of urgency with the year coming to an end.

The conference was being held a few hours out of town. I anticipated engaging with people I didn't know (which felt safe to me) and working on more pain I was ready to get rid of. Over a weekend, it was sure to change my heart. I bought a new journal, made arrangements to be away from work, packed my Bible and my water bottle, and waited for the weekend to arrive.

On the Thursday before the Heart Change weekend, I was in a coffee shop on a break from work and checked my email. There it was—a message from the Heart Change group. I was sure it was a confirmation email describing the details of the weekend ahead. I clicked on it and saw just the opposite. It was a cancelation notice. The Heart Change conference for the weekend had been canceled due to a lack of participants.

I wanted to cry out, "You can't cancel on me. I'm worth it. You can't abandon me; I need a heart change!" I cried instead. I sat there in that coffee shop and wept. I realized right then that I had put a lot of faith in this weekend. I was counting on the program to change my heart, to finalize my healing and wrap up all my work with a bow . . . and they rejected me! (Of course, that was just my feelings talking.)

I texted Barry, "Heart Change was canceled."

He responded back, "That's okay, honey, it was probably meant to be. You can stay home with me now, and I'll take care of you."

He was sweet to say that, but I was thinking, *You don't understand, I've got to go. I was counting on this weekend to heal me, and I need it! What about my heart change?* I felt rejected and a bit desperate, another sign that I wasn't okay. Conferences cancel on people all the time. This felt bigger than that. I was aware that afternoon that abandonment was still at the root of my feelings. I wanted so badly to depend on something or someone and have them stay.

I packed up my laptop and went back to work where I had to set aside my feelings for the evening. I worked the next few hours but was distracted and anxious. It seemed as though my plans and hopes to feel better had been snatched from me. When I got in the car to drive home, I started to form a plan. Heart Change needed to happen for me one way or another. If they weren't going to be there for me, I guess I needed to be there for me (a lesson I was starting to learn that would ultimately be one of my most important lessons of the year). I arrived home to an empty house. Barry was at his Thursday night indoor soccer game. I sat down at the computer and searched for a destination where I could go and change my heart. By the time Barry came through the door, I had booked myself three nights in a cabin in Carson, Washington. Just me, all alone, going for my own Heart Change. I told Barry what I'd done, and he said, "Okay, honey, whatever you need to do." I laid my head on my pillow that night and thought, *I think Barry was right. This was meant to be.*

I woke up the next morning feeling excited about the weekend. I had resigned myself to the fact that I was about to do Heart Change alone and believed that it was going to be a life-changing weekend even without the conference. I packed the car and realized that I was too early to head up the Gorge. My cabin wouldn't be ready until the afternoon. I got on the road anyway and drove to a local coffee shop. I took in my journal and my Bible and started my Heart Change right there. *What better way to start my Heart Change weekend than looking up Scripture about the heart?* I sat with my Bible and my journal and looked up as many verses as I could find. I wrote pages of them . . .

Psalm 19:14 "May these words of my mouth and this meditation of my heart be pleasing in your sight, LORD, my Rock and my Redeemer."

Psalm 51:10,12 "Create in me a pure heart, O God, and renew a steadfast spirit within me. Restore to me the joy of your salvation and grant me a willing spirit, to sustain me."

Jeremiah 29:13 "You will seek me and find me when you seek me with all your heart."

1 Chronicles 28:9 "Serve him with wholehearted devotion and with a willing mind, for the LORD searches every heart and understands every desire and every thought."

Proverbs 3:5–6 "Trust in the LORD with all your heart and lean not on your own understanding; in all your ways submit to him, and he will make your paths straight."

As I searched the Scriptures and wrote, I found myself truly preparing my heart for change and redemption. I knew this weekend was more than a processing weekend to check off the list. I knew it was going to be about opening my heart to truth and healing some places I hadn't looked at for a lifetime. Closing my journal, I grabbed my cup of coffee and headed back to the car to continue my journey. I made a planned stop at Skamania Lodge for lunch, did some more journaling while looking out over the Columbia River Gorge, then continued up to Carson.

When I arrived and saw the setting, peace washed over me. Each cabin was a stand-alone building, nestled among giant evergreen trees looking out over a meadow blanketed with native grasses. The innkeepers, Richard and Theresa, showed me to my cabin, The Salmon Berry. There was a private front porch with a small table, two chairs, and a swinging bench. I opened the door to find a massive king-size log bed, a corner Jacuzzi tub with a luxurious robe hanging close by, and an oversized chair next to the fireplace.

I took a big cleansing breath and started to set up the space for the next few days, laying out my books, journals, pens, and the best-smelling pine candle I could find. I dragged the oversized chair closer to the fireplace, moved a small table next to it, and lit my candle. I stood and looked around the space where I would spend the next three days digging deep, allowing my emotions to be healed and my heart to be changed.

I made myself a cup of hot tea with honey, flipped the switch for the gas fireplace, sat down in my chair, and put a cozy throw on my lap. I picked up a notebook full of notes I had written and resources that Suzy had given me over the months. I flipped to the original paperwork she'd provided at the beginning of the year when she had me catalog stories of my life that had affected me in significant ways. I realized it could be a guide for me as I went through the next few days. My stack of books sat next to me on the ground, and I picked one up that would end up being one of the greatest healing tools of my Heart Change weekend: *The Gift of Inner Healing*[10] by Ruth Carter Stapleton, President Jimmy Carter's sister. I'd read it months earlier and hadn't looked back at it until that day.

It was an old book I had picked up in a secondhand bookstore. Published in 1976, it was dog-eared and scribbled in. Somehow that made it even better. Stapleton did a beautiful job in her book explaining "faith imagination" as a tool for healing. In other words, going back to your memories and reliving them, but this time inviting Jesus into the memory. I was moving through the year believing that time was redemptive and that Jesus is the Great Redeemer, so this process made so much sense to me. She recalled story after story of clients she had counseled who had invited Jesus into painful memories of their past. She told of the healing they'd experienced. I didn't know what to expect from this practice, but I was willing to try.

I said a prayer. *God, show me a specific memory again with particular detail, but this time, allow me to see it with Jesus in the story.* I didn't force the memory or try to control where Jesus was in it . . . I just let the memory come and allowed myself to see Him there with me. One of the most beautiful moments was remembering the day my mom left and using faith imagination to live it over again but see it in a new way.

This time when I was sitting on the curb with my little brother, Mark, waiting for Mom to pick us up, Jesus walked right up behind us and wiggled His way in between the two of us. He sat down on the curb with us and threw His heavy, strong arms around our shoulders and waited with us. I felt warm, safe, and very secure. I allowed myself to sit with that image and be comforted, knowing that He was with me that day and He knew ahead of time just what we would go through. He is the Great Comforter, and He comes close to the brokenhearted. He did that for my little brother and me that day waiting on the curb. That place in front of our house didn't feel so lonely anymore, and it sure didn't feel like my place of abandonment as it had for so long.

As my memory of that day kept playing out, Jesus was there at the ballgame waiting on the bleachers with me as I sat alone, and in the kitchen when the phone rang that night when Mom called to say she wasn't coming home. He went in for the awkward group hug with my brothers, my dad, and me. He held us there as we all cried and were at a loss for words. Jesus was right there with His arms around us. I saw it and I felt it.

As I turned to walk upstairs to go to my bedroom, Jesus followed me up the stairs. When I buried my head into the pillow and sobbed, He sat on the floor and stroked my blond head and began to intercede for me to the Father. He prayed the most beautiful prayer. "Father, will you care for this little girl? She is going to do great things, and we need to keep her safe from harm." He stayed right next to me until I fell asleep.

The memory of that horrible day changed for me. I let myself go to that place in the spiritual world and see what was really happening. I was loved that day, possibly more than any day of my life. I was cared for and prayed for by Jesus Himself. That spring day turned from one of the saddest days of my life to one of the most miraculous. The Redeemer Himself redeemed that day. When I opened my eyes and began to journal about my experience, I was overcome with peace. It's hard to explain, but my heart was changing. I moved through memory after memory just like that. No hurrying and nothing forced. I allowed love to change my story. I allowed love to redeem broken memories and turn them into sacred experiences.

It was beautiful and so real. I didn't rush it. I didn't feel pressure. I just allowed the memories to unfold. I watched Jesus care for me, be there for me, and show me His redeeming and unconditional love. I let the feelings rise to the top and the tears flow. I had nothing to do and no place to be but right there at my Heart Change weekend.

I had so many experiences, big and small, that I worked through and let go of during those few days in Carson. From a cruel statement my second-grade teacher spoke over me to the life-changing moments of my teen years, I went through them, methodically, one at a time. After I followed each memory to the end of the scene, I opened my eyes and journaled about it for a bit. Then, in whatever way I needed to, I processed it, forgave, let go, and put that memory to rest. I got up, stretched, played some music, and spent a few minutes being mindful of the moments. Then I'd sit back down and start with the next memory. It was a gift to know I had time, space, and the ability to do this deep and powerful healing.

With each one of my memories and prayers of faith, I knew I wanted to do something to signify my healing. I love the stories in the Old Testament when altars were built after significant events. Abraham, Noah, Moses, and Joshua— they all built altars of sacrifice, thanks, and dedication to God. I felt the same way. I wanted to do something physical to remember the meaningful experiences I was having.

I built a few altars over the weekend. At one point, I created a little cross to place somewhere private. I walked out on the beautiful grounds, found a couple of twigs, and lashed them together with some long blades of grass. I walked up the hill and pounded the makeshift cross into the ground with a rock under a big fir tree. I took a few minutes and thanked God for what He had just done for me. In the ancient world, the altar was almost exclusively built as a monument to remember or commemorate a divine occurrence that took place at a certain location. I felt like I had a divine occurrence those days in Carson, Washington.

Although I shut the world out for those three days, I still contacted Barry each day to check in and let him know I was okay. I sent him a picture of my cross, waiting to hear back a meaningful response. He texted, "That's nice, honey, but you need to work on your lashings." Always the Eagle Scout.

Heart Change

On my last evening at dusk, the rain was coming down softly. I knew there was a fire pit on the grounds with everything I needed to build a little fire. This "altar" was going to be a place where I burned some of my journaling. I had written about some hard memories over the three days, and I had processed a lot, but I didn't need to keep or read any of it again. I knew burning it would be a significant way to let go of more pain. I put in my earbuds, set my playlist to some of my favorite worship music, and headed to the fire pit.

I used the paper I'd been journaling on for the fire starter. I twisted it up tight, placed a few small sticks over it, and lit it with a match. The rain was coming down and so were my tears. One of my favorite old hymns began to play.

Great is Thy faithfulness, O God my Father
There is no shadow of turning with Thee
Thou changest not, Thy compassions, they fail not
As Thou hast been, Thou forever will be

Great is Thy faithfulness
Great is Thy faithfulness
Morning by morning new mercies I see
All I have needed Thy hand hath provided
Great is Thy faithfulness, Lord, unto me

I was feeling the feelings, lingering in the sadness, then letting go and releasing it all to God. It was a moment I'll always remember. It wasn't easy. Even when I knew letting go would be better for me and my future, holding on felt safe and normal. Letting go meant "normal" had changed. Letting go meant I accepted things as they were. But letting go would also rid my heart of bitterness, resentment, and anger. My heart wanted to be free of those things from my past circumstances and my present.

I took some big breaths, feeling the cool northwest air, and then exhaled long, allowing painful memories to leave. With a feeling of contentment I hadn't felt in months, and tears dripping down my cheeks, I allowed the words of the song to minister to me as I watched the papers crumble and go up in smoke.

I stayed there a while, feeling the sorrow of it all, knowing that I had to feel the pain in order to heal the pain. I was allowing God to restore and redeem parts of me that I hadn't thought about or looked at my whole life. Glancing around to make sure no one was there, I started singing along. "All I have needed Thy hand hath provided. Great is Thy faithfulness, Lord, unto me." I finished the song with rain falling on my head and tears streaming down my face.

I thought when the last paper turned to ashes in the firepit that I could shut off the emotion, close out my ceremony of letting go, and complete my Heart Change weekend, but I couldn't stop crying. Having this time alone and knowing my weekend was coming to an end, I just let the tears come, washing out the loss and the heartache of my teenage years and the reality of how my mom's and dad's choices affected my life. But it was more than that. I slowly moved backward to find a log bench to sit on, not wanting to break the intensity of what was happening. I sobbed about the loss of my long-term friendship and the realization that although good things had come from that relationship, it wasn't good for me, and I was unhealthy in it. I was finally ready to let it go.

My tears started to shift to gratitude, recognizing that the break in that relationship was the catalyst for the depth of emotional healing I'd been experiencing in the last year. I wept at the understanding that every important relationship in my life was better because of the work I'd done and the freedom I was experiencing. I knew I was privileged to have had the time and the resources to invest in my healing. Barry's support and encouragement hadn't waned the entire year, and the love my redeeming ladies had poured into me was so significant to my healing. My tears subsided and I grinned as I thanked God for it all.

I looked around, hoping I was still alone. I'd lost track of time and wasn't paying attention to my surroundings. No one was in sight. I took one final breath and let it out slowly. I turned on my flashlight and made my way back to

The Salmon Berry cabin for the best night's sleep I'd had in a long time.

I got up early the next morning to drive home from my Heart Change weekend. So much went through my head as I drove through the Gorge. I felt lighter, more peaceful, and a whole lot more hopeful. I knew that my weekend wasn't the only reason I was feeling so much better. I had been stringing one good practice together with another for months now. Days with my redeeming ladies, counseling with Suzy, lots of personal reflection time, and now I added to that my Heart Change weekend. I had more redeeming days ahead to make good-time memories, more stories from my past to heal, and more grief to process, but I knew that Heart Change was and would always be one of the most significant and healing weekends of my life.

Keep Going,
It's Going to Be Worth It

Karen was training to climb Mount St. Helens, and I was about to be in training with her. Hiking in the Pacific Northwest was on the agenda for this redeeming day. Karen inspired me with her domestic abilities, but her physical strength and adventurous spirit were even more impressive. The hiking group she belonged to invited novice hikers to experience the trails with them. Despite having little experience, I was about to hike in the Columbia River Gorge.

Karen and I planned the hike ahead of time so I could get prepared—mentally as well as physically. I needed some hiking shoes. I went to the local shoe store, When the Shoe Fits, and asked them to show me the best hiking shoe they had. I tried on four or five pairs until I found the perfect shoe. I walked out of the store that day with the most comfortable hiking shoe they had, and I wore them around the house for the next twelve hours to break them in.

We met early on Saturday morning in a church parking lot, and I met my fellow climbers. The leader of the group was an experienced hiker and had led groups for years. The first thing he did after meeting me was look down at my shoes and say, "Oh boy . . . new shoes." He was probably envisioning carrying me the last mile.

We got into a few rigs and caravanned up the Gorge, planning to climb Dog Mountain. When we got to the trail-head, there wasn't one empty parking spot. It was a popular hike and you had to get there early in the morning to get a spot. We turned back and opted for a hike about five miles back—Cape Horn. It was my lucky day, but I didn't know it. Dog Mountain wouldn't have been a good "first" for me or my new shoes.

We arrived at the trailhead, parked, and moved out. We started up the trail, and I was surprised at how fast every-body moved. Weren't we going to stop and visit? Didn't we have time for a few photos? I guess not. Karen stayed close by. I knew she could have been leading the pack, but she wouldn't leave me behind.

She whispered, "Letha, being in the back of the pack is a bad place to be. When the group stops for a little rest to wait for the slower ones, the minute the last hiker catches up, they head out again. If you hang back there, you'll never get a rest."

"So, what do I do?"

She said, "Let's move up."

And so we did. Karen gently said, "Passing on the left." And the two of us passed by a few of our group and put ourselves in the middle of the pack instead of the back. I worked hard to keep up with her, and I did pretty well. Karen was proud of me. She turned back to check on me. "I'm impressed. I thought you might struggle to keep up with us."

Every once in a while, the leader would call out, "Hey, New Shoes, how ya doing?"

I'd smile and say, "I'm walking on clouds." They were really good shoes.

I kept the pace in the middle of the group and was even bold enough to ask if I could go out in front of the pack so I could take some pictures of the trail. I got some incredible photos of the most beautiful blue flowers strewn along both sides of the winding trail. They were magnificent. It's a good thing I got the photos because I didn't get to stop and look at the scenery for long.

We did break for a quick lunch at a beautiful amphi-theater looking out over the Gorge. It was breathtaking.

The Gorge is a place of spectacular natural beauty. The steep canyon walls rise to more than 4,000 feet above the river in some places. I could see waterfalls and evergreen trees for miles. The morning fog was lifting, and the sun was casting light on the Oregon side. One of the hikers had prepared a little devotional, so, as we ate our lunch, he shared it with us. He read 2 Timothy 1:7—"For the Spirit God gave us does not make us timid, but gives us power, love and self-discipline."

Karen looked over at me from across the circle when he read it, and smiled. I smiled back. We both knew that I was experiencing that power, love, and self-discipline, and it was healing me. I was healing the past, which took courage, but I was also making choices in my present day to have healthier relationships. "Feel the fear and do it anyway" could have been my mantra as I moved through the year, so that Scripture seemed meant just for me that Saturday afternoon.

We finished our short lunch break and continued up the trail. The second half seemed steeper and more rugged. I'm not sure if it really was or if I was physically tired from the steps I had taken to get me this far. All of a sudden, hikers started passing us on their way back down the trail. We hugged the inside of the path as they passed on the outside. One girl with a spring in her step and a smile on her face looked right at me, and seeing I was sweating and winded, said, "Keep going, it's going to be worth it."

I could have started sobbing right then, not because my feet hurt or because I was tired due to the hike, but because that was just the encouragement I needed in my personal journey to continue to heal and recover from my pain. I wanted to stop and thank her, but our hiking group was relentless. I wanted to tell her about my plan to redeem lost time and tell her what she said was true and I believed it. It was worth it, and I knew it. The pain, the labor, and the never-ending processing were worth it because the view on top would be something I'd never get to experience if not for the work to get there.

I had no promise at the beginning of the year that if I worked this hard for some calculated amount of time, I'd feel better. It was a slow, steady, and sometimes very difficult decision to keep moving forward. Many times throughout the year, I had thought about how much easier it would be to just turn around. To just go back to the ways things always were and get my needs met again by people outside of myself. But I trusted the process and just kept moving forward, one step at a time. Sometimes, one baby step at a time.

We finally got to the top of the trail, and it was worth it. The scene from across the river was extraordinary. Larch Mountain, the bare knob of Angel's Rest, and Multnomah Falls were in view. The tears that I'd been holding back since I passed the hiker on the trail, started to fall. I'm sure the hiking group thought my feet hurt or something when they looked over and saw me crying. Karen came over to the edge where I stood, slipped her arm around me, and didn't speak. She was aware of my feelings and wanted me to know without saying a word that she was there for me. I allowed myself time. As I looked out, I thought about not just the splendor of God's creation and the beauty of the Columbia River Gorge, but also of my own journey of healing and how far I'd come.

After a couple of photos and a few more minutes to take in the view, we turned back to head down the trail. It was all I could do to not cry the whole way down as I passed people coming up and I got to say to them, "Keep going, it's going to be worth it."

21

Christmas at the Mansion

The power to grow and heal came from looking back and being curious about my story, then recognizing I had the power to redeem it. Many might say, *What's the point of looking back or dwelling on the past?* William Faulkner wrote in his book, *Requiem for a Nun,* "The past isn't dead . . . it's not even past."[11] I came to understand just what he meant throughout the year of my redemption. My past had everything to do with how I thought and what made me tick. My final redeeming day with Kristi would allow me another opportunity to look back.

Kristi and I made plans to tour the Pittock Mansion in Portland, knowing it was decorated for the holidays. I had some lonely Christmases as an adolescent, so this seemed like another therapeutic way for me to go back in time and heal some memories that I hadn't thought about for years. I knew touring the Pittock's home would allow me the opportunity to recollect the past, I just didn't expect so many other feelings to come up.

We arrived at the mansion and stood in a short line to purchase our tickets. Kristi reached over and put her hand on my shoulder. "How are you feeling about the holiday season? I know when you're grieving, holidays can be hard."

"Yes, they can, but I'm doing better every day. I feel like I'm in such a different place than I was last Christmas. This time last year I was feeling waves of despair over my lost friendship with Ruth. I hadn't started counseling yet and was just beginning the process of letting go. I've processed a lot since then." I put my hand on her hand and gave it a little squeeze. "Kristi, thank you for your friendship and for being bold enough to ask difficult questions. I'm not afraid of these kinds of conversations like I was a year ago. So much has changed for me."

"I'm so glad. Getting to know you better and being a part of this journey has been significant for me. I'll never forget this year."

"Neither will I," I said with a smile.

We bought our tickets to enter, and I stood and read the placard outside the door before entering.

The Pittock Mansion was originally built in 1914 and was a private home for the Oregonian newspaper's publisher Henry Pittock and his wife, Georgiana. It has forty-six rooms and a panoramic view of downtown Portland. Georgiana was an avid gardener who was a founding member of the Portland Rose Society, hosted the first Portland Rose Show in 1889, and helped launch the Portland Rose Festival. The mansion is surrounded by formal gardens that reflect her passion for gardening.

It was a magnificent place, and especially beautiful at Christmas. We walked through the home, imagining the lives of the families who lived there. A few generations of the Pittock family had grown up in that home, and I couldn't help but think about the stories (both good and bad) passed down from generation to generation. On our tour, we heard tales of parties and celebrations, as well as stories of sickness and sorrow—all the stories that make up the life of a family.

My stomach clenched when we were shown the "sick porch" where the Pittocks would quarantine their family members who contracted tuberculosis, or consumption. Through much of the 1800s, consumptive patients sought the cure to these illnesses through rest and a colder climate. The porches were also a way to prevent the sick person from spreading their illness to other members of the family. I stood there looking at the porch with its floor-to-ceiling windows and sparse furnishings, considering the reality of what I was hearing. The Pittocks were a multigenerational family living under that roof, so that meant parents and grandparents, aunts and uncles, and, sadly, children were all a part of the narrative of the person left to "heal" on that sick porch. Oh, if walls could talk, what stories would I have heard on that winter afternoon walking through the home of the Pittock family?

I strolled through the mansion thinking about my story. The narrative of my family's life had many scenes, good ones and bad ones, just like the Pittocks. As I went from room to room, looking at the ornately decorated Christmas trees, my mind kept taking me back to one Christmas with my little brother, Mark.

It was Christmas Day 1974. Holidays were a hard thing at our house after mom left. I was the one who had to rally the troops to create any kind of celebration. Dad provided the charge card, but my brothers and I had to provide the magic. There's not much magic when you buy your own Christmas gifts. I would wrap the gifts for the boys, and I would even wrap mine so I'd have something to open on Christmas morning.

In the past, my older married siblings would all come

to our house on Christmas Day to open presents and have dinner. Not anymore. The glue that held our family together wasn't there anymore. Christmas didn't sparkle like it used to. It's no wonder I go to extremes during the holidays now. Every one of them.

This Christmas, Joey had his driver's license and Dad was dating. Joey had been invited to his girlfriend's home for the day, and Dad was invited to his. That left Mark and me at home. In 1974 there was no cable TV to watch, no Christmas DVDs to play, and *The Christmas Story* with Ralphie wasn't looping on a marathon for twenty-four hours. Mark and I hung out in the living room by the Christmas tree for a while after Dad left, warmed up some leftovers, and then tried to find something to watch on TV.

Thinking back, I ask myself questions like, *Why didn't we go with Dad?* or *Why didn't Dad plan something in advance, knowing we'd be left alone?* I always come back to the same answer. People do what they need to do to get their needs met. Sometimes, depending on the need, those choices are selfish. My dad was suffering. He was rejected and betrayed. He was treating his wounds the only way he knew how, by seeking another relationship. Although I forgave Mom and Dad, I was careful to not justify my parents' behavior. For me to heal and change my future, I was responsible for naming the harm that had been done to me. Rather than blame anyone for their actions, it was important for me to engage my heart and accept the harm that I experienced.

I also think about my older siblings. *Where were they on Christmas Day? Why weren't we invited over to their homes? Why wasn't anyone looking out for my little brother and me?*

I answer those questions, too, because I know now what it's like to raise a family and make memories. My siblings were living their lives with their children and creating traditions for themselves. I know they didn't purposely neglect us; they were focused, and rightly so, on their own lives. That left Mark and me home alone on Christmas Day.

Remember Helen Reddy's song, "You and Me Against the World"? Well, Mark and I had given each other our own nicknames, Mar and La. We looked at each other at some point in the day and started to sing, "Mar and La against the world, sometimes it feels like Mar and La against the world." We laughed, but it wasn't funny. We were doing what we needed to do to ease our pain: connecting with each other and acting silly.

Mark is still silly. He's the baby of the family and he's the lampshade guy. I can't help but think about how much of his personality today goes all the way back to those days when being silly, laughing, and making jokes eased his pain. He used comedy to cope; I made things look good. We both followed through in our adult lives with the roles we played all those years ago. We had pain and shame, and we covered it up with humor and control.

There's nothing wrong with being funny. In fact, Mark still makes me laugh and can tell a story better than anyone I know. He's also one of the most creative and innovative people I've ever met. He's got skills, and I'm always impressed with how he can take nothing and turn it into something great. He has done that since he was a little boy.

I can create an event, make it beautiful, and control it down to the toothpick. My friends and family have benefited from my "skill" too. There's no question that Mark and I became who we are because of the experiences we had.

I learned to look at every one of those experiences from a redemptive perspective. Mark and I wouldn't be who we are today without the pain of our childhoods. We wouldn't influence the people we influence without those experiences that made us who we are. The purpose of my healing was not to lose the gifts and talents I gained because of my painful upbringing, but to use them in healthy ways for me and my family and for the generations to come.

Mark and I still sing that song sometimes when we're together. He laughs and I usually cry. My little brother and I have traveled through a lot of life together since that day we were left on the curb. I made a short video card for his sixtieth birthday, and I sang our song, "Mar and La against the world, sometimes it feels like Mar and La against the world." I cried when I filmed it; rumor has it, he cried when he watched it.

If I made a storyboard of my life, I would see all the twists and turns that became the meaningful and influential parts of my story. I'd see how the people and the experiences I had mattered and, quite frankly, made me who I am today. Even that Christmas Day spent alone with my little brother.

This year had been a time of reckoning for me. It was a time to take the story of my life seriously and become curious about how it unfolded and what effect it had on me. With the exception of the genes that were passed on to me, how I thought was entirely a function of the experiences I had in my life. I came to understand over the year that engaging my story and being brutally honest with others and myself was the only way I was going to change the way I thought or have any permanent healing. Honesty required that I named how life really was for me, and honesty required that I named how I was hurt. I had to look at how my mom hurt me, and I had to look at how my dad hurt me.

I learned that people who know themselves and have a heightened capacity for self-reflection have much more empathy than others. Engaging my story was in no way a selfish endeavor. In fact, I found that the more I addressed the wounded parts of my heart, the better I related and the more I loved others.

At first, I struggled to look back and didn't want to blame my parents. I came to understand that there's a difference between blaming someone and naming what has been true about your relationship with them. I wanted to love my parents well and forgive them. I knew that began with naming what had been true about how I related to my parents and how my parents related to me. Disclaiming my experiences with my mom and dad was really disowning my life. I gained nothing by closing my eyes to the truth of my relationship with them. It didn't change my story to excuse their behavior, just as it didn't change my story to blame them. My story was just my story.

The point of engaging my past was so I could live well in the present. It sounds a bit ironic, but until I engaged my story, I was actually living as much in the past as I was in the present. Looking back at my story and the experiences that wounded me allowed me to heal and become much more of who I was intended to be in the present. Had I denied myself that opportunity, I would still be identifying, thinking, and acting like an abandoned little girl. What was the point of me dwelling in my past?. . . So I could live fully in the present. The layers of healing that were happening for me, from my experiences with faith imagination to my forgiveness work, were changing my past, and that had everything to do with my future.

After touring every inch of the mansion, imagining the lives of the families that lived there, and enjoying the gorgeous Christmas decorations, Kristi and I finished our time outside in the gardens. They were a sight to see, even in the winter. We promised each other we'd come back in the spring when the grounds would be in full bloom.

We made it back over the interstate bridge before traffic got too busy and chose a nice restaurant in downtown Vancouver to have lunch. The year was winding down, and I was happy to share more of my healing and my experiences with Kristi. She had become a trusted friend. I always felt known after I spent the day with Kristi. She was a great listener and always reminded me of the growth she saw in me.

I had one more redeeming day to go—one more opportunity to redeem lost time with women who chose to stand in the gap. A year had passed since I wrote a letter to those four friends asking if they could help me make time good again. What a difference a year can make.

22

I Am Redeemed

I agreed to meet Ruth for dinner. We hadn't spoken in over a year, and I needed closure on the breakup of our friendship. I drove to the restaurant feeling relaxed. My hands were loose on the steering wheel and my heartbeat was calm and steady. Earlier in the year she had reached out to see if we could get together, but I wasn't ready. The thought of seeing her caused me anxiety, so I knew it wasn't the right time. This night felt totally different.

She was waiting in the lobby when I arrived, and we greeted each other with a hug. With a warm voice and caring tone, I whispered, "Hello, it's good to see you."

"It's good to see you too," she said with a smile. We followed the hostess back and were seated in a booth. As we looked over the menu, we chatted casually.

I can only describe our meeting as a spiritual experience. I went from feeling deep pain about the loss of our friendship months earlier to sitting across from Ruth feeling extremely peaceful. With unhurried speech, I shared a bit of the journey I'd been on in the last year. She caught me up on her life too. Instead of feeling rejected and betrayed, as I did the last time I saw her, I felt calm and compassionate. I experienced the scene unfolding as if I were hovering over the table watching it. I was gentle as I spoke, telling her what I had learned about my unhealthiness in our relationship without judging her. I was well aware that the healing work I'd focused on my thirteen-year-old self was significant and had changed me. We walked out of the restaurant together two hours later and said goodbye at the curb. There wasn't a conversation about a next time, and I was glad about that. Although the evening had been comfortable, reconciliation of our friendship was not my desire.

I drove home feeling a depth of freedom and peace I hadn't known in a long time.

The following week, my redeeming ladies met together at Nancy's home for one final redeeming day as a group. They hadn't seen one another since our spring luncheon but felt connected through my monthly emails and the commitment they made to me the previous year. We were all bound together by love and a common focus—redemption.

As I was getting ready that morning, I couldn't help but think about the stark contrast between how I was feeling this redeeming day, and how I felt twelve months earlier on the morning of my first one. I think it's true that time heals, but I believe it's truer that love heals. I was the recipient of great love from others and, maybe more importantly, from myself. I also believe it's not time alone that heals, but what you do with the time that makes the difference. I had used time, weaved together with truth and grace, and I was a changed person.

At the beginning of this journey, I felt desperate, empty, and broken. I pressed on through the months with my plan of redeeming my adolescence not because I was feeling better with each step, but because I trusted the process. Time was experience, and I had the ability to step back into time, where I had been removed years ago, and make it good. And that's exactly what I did.

I had done important work over the last year redeeming my childhood, but I was also growing in my current experiences as healing took place in my life. I was consistently visiting my mom, even through the hardest weeks in my counseling. I remember during one appointment Suzy suggested that I might take a break from my weekly visits to see my mom. She let me know that it would be okay to skip a few weeks when I was doing some of my most difficult healing regarding Mom. I never did need to take a break. I credit that to the forgiveness work I had done so many years earlier. I was able, even on the days when I wept through my entire counseling appointment, to drop by my mom's care facility on the way home. I'd take some flowers, maybe a milkshake, and before I'd leave, I would wipe her face with a warm lavender water washcloth, sometimes weeping as I did it. Somehow as I continued to redeem the time my mom had taken from me, I was able to love her even more.

Good time had accumulated in the year of my redemption, and I was on my way this last month of the year to celebrate with the women who helped me do it: my redeeming ladies. Time is experience, and I knew what that meant now. With the help of my friends, I had redeemed some painful time and made it good.

When I arrived at Nancy's, everyone was there. Nancy had decorated the table exquisitely. The centerpiece sparkled, casting glints of light off the shiny place settings. I saw my name inscribed in fancy script on a place card indicating my seat.

The five of us sat and reminisced about the year as we shared a meal. From my place at the head of the table, I looked from face to beautiful face.

Nancy had ushered internal order back into my life.

She not only gave of her time but showed me through her example that peace on the inside reflects on the outside.

Karen had shown me motherly love. Her giving spirit helped me heal from feelings of unworthiness, and she showed me I was worthy of good and beautiful things.

Judy was a lover of life and had taught me how to live in the present moment. She had been a bright light in the past year, reminding me of a redemptive perspective in even the most painful seasons of life.

Kristi exhibited exquisite attention to detail in everything she did. Her devotion and care throughout the year helped me feel loved.

All my redeeming ladies took their roles in my redemption plan very seriously. They were great instructors as well as great listeners. They showed me love and tenderness while I healed, and they were trustworthy guides and mentors. I knew the long-term impact of their commitment was life-changing for me, and I had a feeling it was going to be for them as well. They accepted me as I was but also encouraged me to grow and persevere in my quest for healing. They were like loving moms should be.

It is rare to find women who are so capable, living their own lives to the fullest and yet still able to give of themselves for others. I found four of them who freely and lovingly gave and sacrificed their time for me. For that I will be eternally grateful.

After dessert, we moved over to the living room to exchange gifts and finish our coffee. I wanted to give a small token to my sweet friends who had poured so much love and time into me the past year. That had not been an easy gift to find. I found beautiful little glass boxes and had "Redeemed" etched on the top of each one. I also included a handwritten note inside for each of them. I read each personal love note out loud while we sat together opening our gifts. I cried through each one, so grateful for redemption and for the role each one of my redeeming ladies played in the process of my healing. We said our final goodbyes, but we all agreed we were going to keep the "band" together. The bond that had been created this year would not be easily broken.

I drove home in silence. I was flooded with memories and feelings, not only from our afternoon spent together but also from the year. I thought back to the beginning of the year, about choosing the word *redeemed* and the plan that was orchestrated from start to finish. I was so glad I had been brave enough to ask these women to participate in my redemption plan, knowing they would follow through and walk beside me as I healed.

All year long God was working out the story of the cross in my life. He redeemed me, He restored me, and He caused me to triumph. I was a willing participant, and a faithful one at that, but He gave me strength that allowed me to keep taking one step after another, even when I didn't feel like it. He took a wounded little girl and turned her into a healed, beautiful woman.

From my creative plan to redeem time with my friends and make time good again, to the hard work of healing past wounds and learning to take tender loving care of myself, I was a different person. I went from feeling like an abandoned little girl looking outside of myself to get my needs met, to a confident woman who now trusted herself and her ability to make good decisions about friendships. I discovered that I could be my own best friend. As cliché as that sounds, it might have been the most important thing I learned all year. I changed the way I identified with myself. Before, I had identified with titles like abandoned and rejected, and now I was living redeemed and accepted. I stepped out of my history instead of continuing to live in it and allowing it to define me.

I learned that it is never too late to open up to those who love and care for us. I learned that just because I missed out on some important development as an adolescent, it didn't mean I couldn't grow up now and be transformed. I worked through trust issues, boundaries, forgiveness, and the separation issues caused by my abandonment. Grace, truth, and time worked together to give me a second chance.

Through my faith and my participation in the difficult process of facing my past, God healed my soul. I am now sure I will always be alright . . . no matter who rejects me, what betrayal I might feel, and even if I were to be abandoned again. I know I'll never be alone because I have everything I need right inside of me.

I am redeemed.

Epilogue

As I was writing this book and retelling the story of redeeming my adolescence, I was spending the last days of my mom's life with her. She passed away before I finished this story. She was ninety-six years old when she slipped from this earth.

To say I am grateful for the healing work I had done surrounding the story of my mom and our fractured relationship would be a giant understatement. I was able, for years and through the last days of her life, to offer her the tender loving care that a daughter's heart would hope to offer her mother. I was able to offer her what she wasn't able to offer me. I stayed. I cared for her even on my hardest days. I didn't abandon or reject her even when it got hard for me. I was able to attune to her feelings the way she was unable to attune to mine. I was able to give her what my heart longed for from her.

My relationship with my mom and my ability to show loving care to her throughout her life wasn't birthed out of any apology or request for forgiveness on her part. She never spoke of her choice to abandon us or the harm she caused my siblings or me. For years, I hoped I would hear the words, "I'm so sorry for leaving you, honey," but at some point, I recognized that she was never going to speak those words or offer any kind of remorse. Mom's pain and regret were buried deep inside her, and she never chose to dig them up or heal the wounded places in her soul.

My decision to forgive my mom didn't make her actions acceptable to me, but forgiveness allowed me the peace to accept and love her. The choice I made to forgive my mom and continue the work of healing my adolescence was the greatest gift I've ever received, and I gave it to myself. My choice to be curious, engage my story, and recognize who I had become because of my past changed every relationship in my life, starting with the one I have with myself.

I was honored to be the one to give the eulogy at Mom's memorial service. I spoke of her life—the love and the pain. I told of her many gifts and talents and her creative personality, but mostly I spoke of her legacy, her eight children, and all her children's children. She left behind a family who will now have to choose to forgive with her gone. I hope for the sake of all the generations that follow us that we all will continue to do the life-giving work of engaging our individual stories and healing our pasts. In spite of the pain, redemption is possible.

Take it from someone who knows.

Letha with her brothers
Mark and Joey, 1973

Letha and Barry as
high-school seniors

Letha with her mom,
graduation day, 1977

Letha and Barry

Letha and her
son, Bennett

Bennett and his
wife, Crystal

Letha with her sisters
left to right: Linda, Nancy, Diane, and Vickie

Letha with her siblings

The Redeeming Ladies

Nancy   Judy

Kristi   Karen

Letha's last redeeming day, at Nancy's house

Letha with her redeeming ladies

Acknowledgments

I could not have undertaken this journey without many special people.

I want to express my deepest gratitude for my redeeming ladies, who invested so much of themselves to create "good time" experiences for me. Judy, Karen, Kristi, and Nancy—I'll be forever indebted to you for the love and devotion you showed me the year of my redemption. This book wouldn't be in existence without the four of you. I have a feeling this "band" is going stay together for a long time.

Wendy, if not for your *strong* encouragement that fateful day at the coffee shop, I wouldn't have started writing this book. You challenged me to live without regrets and inspired courage in me to tell my story. Thank you for believing in me. I'm extremely grateful for your encouragement and friendship.

To my sisters Linda, Diane, Nancy, and Vickie—thank you for your reassurance as I wrote my story. When I felt trepidation about being vulnerable, you were there to usher in peace and encourage me to forge ahead. Your loving support made such a difference. And especially Diane—without your help, I'd still be trying to organize my thoughts. You have my deepest thanks for the countless hours you spent reading and re-reading my manuscript, proofing and proofing again, and helping me with every part of this process. One of the benefits of writing this book was spending more time with you.

To my Book Club Sisters—inquiring minds want to know, and you always wanted to know. "How's your book coming along? When will it be done? When do we get to read it?" Thank you for inquiring. Thank you for holding me accountable to the task. I love reading with you.

Thank you to my Healthy Weigh family, who were open to learning about healing their souls while I was healing mine.

Sincere thanks to my editor, Sarah Barnum of Trailblaze Editorial. Sarah, thank you for your incredible feedback, guidance, and editorial expertise. You challenged me to improve my writing skills and helped me tell a much better story. Your ability to correct writing errors while also assessing the whole story was impressive. I'm so thankful.

Tisha Martin, thank you for your keen eyes, giving my manuscript one final proofing.

Acknowledgments

Madison, it means so much to me to have your artistry on the cover of my book. You took the time to create more than just a beautiful picture—it's a memory. I'm so grateful that you shared your talent with me.

Bennett, from the day you told me it wasn't too late to heal my adolescence, you've been invested in my journey. You listened and cared about my emotional healing and were a proponent of me writing a book about it. You and Crystal have stayed curious and maintained enthusiasm throughout this long writing project. (Bless you.) I'm so thankful for you. I love you.

Barry, without your continued love and support, I might not have followed through with my redeeming plan. You offered me the space and time I needed to heal and then to write about it. You were always there to remind me of the truth and extended grace to me as I slowly and painfully took the steps necessary to heal my past. Thank you for always caring so much about my story. I love you more today than yesterday . . .

Jesus, all I have needed thy hand hath provided. Thank you for whispering to me. Thank you for loving me. You are my Redeemer, the author and finisher of my story.

Endnotes

Chapter Two

1. Dr. Henry Cloud, *Changes that Heal: Four Practical Steps to a Happier, Healthier You* (Grand Rapids: Zondervan, 2018).
2. *A Few Good Men,* directed by Rob Reiner (Beverly Hills: Castle Rock Entertainment, 1992).

Chapter Five

3. Dr. Henry Cloud and John Townsend, *Safe People: How to Find Relationships that are Good for You and Avoid Those that Aren't* (Grand Rapids: Zondervan, 1996).

Chapter Eight

4. Melody Beattie, *Codependent No More: How to Stop Controlling Others and Start Caring for Yourself* (New York: Spiegel and Grau, 2022).

Chapter Eleven

5. Margaret Paul, PhD, *Inner Bonding: Becoming a Loving Adult to Your Inner Child* (San Francisco: Harper One, 1992).

Chapter Twelve

6. Mark Nepo, *The Book of Awakening: Having the Life You*

Want by Being Present to the Life You Have (Newburyport: Red Wheel, 2020), 29.

7. Julia Cameron, *The Artist's Way: A Spiritual Path to Higher Creativity* (Chicago: Souvenir Press, 2020), 18.

Chapter Fifteen

8. John M. Gottman and Nan Silver, *The Seven Principles for Making Marriage Work: A Practical Guide from the Country's Foremost Relationship Expert* (New York: Harmony, 2015), 42.

Chapter Eighteen

9. George Santayana, *The Life of Reason: The Phases of Human Progress* (Amherst: Prometheus Books, 1998), 83.

Chapter Nineteen

10. Stapleton, Ruth Carter. *The Gift of Inner Healing* (Waco: Word Book Publishers, 1977).

Chapter Twenty-One

11. Faulkner, William. *Requiem for a Nun* (New York: Vintage International, 1951), 7.

Made in United States
Troutdale, OR
02/21/2025

29154104R00148